# STORIES of NORWAY

D1421944

## John A. Yilek

# Wasteland Press

www.wastelandpress.net
Shelbyville, KY USA

*Stories of Norway*
by John A. Yilek

First Printing – February 2017
ISBN: 978-1-68111-168-1
Library of Congress Control Number: 2017933035

Printed in the U.S.A.

0    1    2    3    4    5

# CONTENTS

# CHAPTER ONE:
# A Norwegian Chieftain
# in Ancient Times

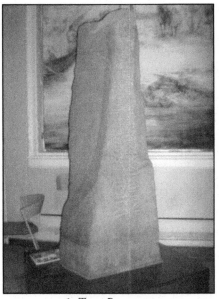

*1. Tune Runestone*

WODURID WAS A MIGHTY CHIEFTAIN who lived east of the Oslofjord in southeast Norway, hundreds of years before the age of the Vikings. In about AD 400 he died and was buried in a grave mound at Tune. Traces of his story are told in the Tune Runestone, which was carved in his honor and raised atop the burial mound or in another visible place. There were already other grave mounds at Tune, which had been a seat of Norwegian chieftains for centuries.

The Tune stone contains one of the longest and most important inscriptions of any Norwegian runestone that was written in the ancient Scandinavian language of Proto-Norse by use of a runic script of 24 characters called Elder Futhark. The Norwegians and other Scandinavians carved runes in Proto-Norse and Elder Futhark during the period from about AD 180 to 600. Thereafter, the language and characters gradually evolved into Old Norse, the language of the Vikings, and into a shorter set of 16 runic symbols called Younger Futhark. Runes were usually carved on stones, weapons, tools, jewelry, or medallions.

After many centuries, the Tune stone was found in 1627 in a churchyard at Tune, where it had been built into a cemetery wall, presumably at the same burial site. Later the stone was moved to Oslo, and it is now standing in the University Museum of Cultural History.

For well over a hundred years, runologists have been trying to decipher the inscription on both sides of the Tune stone. Part of the problem is that the top edge of the stone is broken off and lost, and some runes are missing. The text is read alternately from right to left, left to right, and up and down. There are no spaces between the words. Furthermore, Proto-Norse was a complex language with many lengthy words in different variations and sequences. Consequently, the runic experts have come up with different translations of the text. Our story is based on some of the most recent interpretations of the Tune stone.

When Wodurid was born, he was given a name that meant "the furious horseman". The Norse god Odin was also called the furious horseman as he rode his magnificent eight-legged steed named Sleipnir into battle. So Wodurid was apparently named after Odin, and he was expected to be a wise chieftain, a brave warrior, and a religious leader. After he succeeded his father as chieftain, Wodurid and his band of professional fighters and bodyguards (called the *hird*) protected his many subjects, primarily farmers, from other chieftains and tribes, including foreign Germanic tribes that invaded Norway from the east. In return for that protection, the farmers and other subjects paid tribute to the chieftain, usually in the form of farm products, and they extended him their loyalty.

Wodurid lived at the beginning of a violent period called the Age of Migration, when the dreaded Huns attacked the Germanic people, and several Germanic tribes moved around Europe in search of a better and safer homeland. A few of those tribes, including the *horder* and the *ryger* from Germany, pushed into Norway, attacking the existing Norwegians and establishing their own kingdoms in various parts of the country.

In about AD 550 the Gothic historian Jordanes, in his work entitled *The Origin and Deeds of the Goths* (or *Getica*), identified various groups of people in Norway who were ruled by their own kings or chieftains. Those groups included the raumarici (*raumer*) around the Oslofjord, the taetel (*teler*) in Telemark, the augandzi (*egder*) in Agder, the rugi (ryger) in Rogaland, the arochi (horder) in Hordaland, the ranii (*raumi*) in Romsdal, and the adogit (*haløyger*) in Northern Norway. Jordanes described the Norwegians as tall and spirited warriors who fought like cruel, wild beasts.

Apart from being a brave warrior, Wodurid was a very wealthy person who owned much land and other property. As early as the Bronze Age, which lasted from 1800 to 500 BC in Norway, Norwegian chieftains had increased their wealth by building large boats that could be rowed all the way across the Skagerrak to marketplaces in Denmark. There they traded their products from Norway in exchange for valuable weapons, jewelry, and other goods from many lands.

Bronze Age rock carvings at Skjeberg near Tune contain drawings of boats that were used for this purpose over hundreds of years. The vessels were rowed without sails by large crews of rowers, and they were constructed with unique double bows and sterns where both the keel and the gunwales extended beyond the front and back of the hull. An example of this type of craft is the *Hjortspring* boat that was recovered from a marsh on the island of Als in Denmark. The boat was built in about 350 BC, and it looked very similar to the double-prow boats in the Skjeberg rock carvings.

In AD 98 the Roman historian Cornelius Tacitus wrote a book called *Germania* in which he described the Germanic tribes of Europe, including the Scandinavians. He was impressed by the ships, chieftains, and warriors of the Suiones who lived in Scandinavia across the sea from Denmark. They had powerful fleets of ships without sails, and each ship had a prow at each end so it could be rowed or beached in either direction. Their armies and weapons were formidable, and their chieftains were very wealthy men who commanded absolute obedience from their followers. A rich, well-respected chieftain like Wodurid fit well within that description.

Shipbuilding, seafaring, and trade continued to be important into the Viking age (AD 789 to 1066), as shown by the *Tune* ship in the Viking Ship Museum in Oslo. The *Tune* ship was buried in a grave mound at Tune along with a Viking warrior and his horses and weapons. The warrior could have been one of Wodurid's distant descendants.

Wodurid was also a family man. Even though he had no sons who survived him, he spent time with his wife, three daughters, and grandchildren, all of whom were devoted to him. So he combined the roles of chieftain, warrior, religious leader, wealthy property owner, husband, father, and grandfather.

In Proto-Norse society, when a chieftain died, his oldest son became the new chieftain and the owner of his father's lands and other property. However, since Wodurid had no surviving sons, his three daughters inherited his property when he died. As the closest heirs of the chieftain, the daughters were also responsible for preparing and hosting the funeral feast. Wodurid's family, friends, and hird attended the feast, and enjoyed fine food and drink while seated around the hearth in Wodurid's longhouse and ceremonial hall.

After the burial of Wodurid's body along with rich grave goods in the burial mound, and the celebration of the funeral feast, it was customary for another member of Wodurid's family to carve and raise a runestone in his honor, so he could be remembered as a great chieftain and a courageous warrior. In Wodurid's case, the person who carved the Tune stone was a man named Wiw, who may have been the chieftain's grandson. As his oldest grandson, Wiw could also have inherited some of Wodurid's lands and other property, and he became the new chieftain and leader of the hird and all the farmers and other people around Tune.

Wiw carved the Tune stone and placed it on the burial mound or another visible place as a memorial to Wodurid, but also as a record of the inheritance rights and duties of the family members. The inscription on the stone reads: "I, Wiw, in memory of Wodurid, lord, carved these runes. I dedicated the stone to Wodurid. Three daughters, the most loving and closest of the heirs, prepared the funeral feast."

The Tune Runestone not only tells the story of a chieftain and his family. In addition, it is evidence of a well-organized, ancient Norwegian society in which the ruler, his family, the hird, and the local farmers and other subjects all played important roles, and there were already established rules of property ownership and inheritance in Norway.

# CHAPTER TWO:
# *Rigsthula –*
# *The Song of Rig*

*2. Viking longhouse at Avaldsnes*

THE SONG OF RIG (*RIGSTHULA*) is a poem by an unknown author, perhaps a wandering minstrel. It was originally composed in Old Norse, most likely in the 10th century, and it was sung for hundreds of years before being written down in a form that survives to the present day. The ending and a few other verses are missing from the written version. The song tells the story of a Norse god named Rig who fathered the human race. Although it is obviously a fictional account, the poem is considered to be an accurate depiction of Norwegian society in Viking times.

During the age of the Vikings (AD 789 to 1066), Norwegians and their descendants attacked the British Isles and Europe, traded goods and established settlements in many lands, and explored the North Atlantic Ocean all the way to North America. Back home in Norway, there was a stratified agricultural society that was divided into an upper class of aristocrats, a middle class of other freemen, and a lower class of slaves.

The members of the upper class were kings, jarls (earls), other chieftains, and their families and closest companions. They had the most wealth, owned vast lands and other property, wore the finest clothing, enjoyed the best food and furnishings, and lived in the largest longhouses, some of which were big enough to contain ceremonial halls. The king, jarl, or chieftain was the political and military leader of all the people in his part of Norway. Many noblemen owned ships and commanded armies of Vikings that attacked and traded throughout Europe. The ruler also presided at religious ceremonies and the ting, which was a periodic gathering of all the freemen in the area to make rules, settle disputes, and prosecute criminals. Some of the noblemen claimed that they could trace their ancestry back to the gods.

The other freemen and their families made up the middle class. Most of them were farmers who owned or leased their farms, but there were other freemen who were merchants, craftsmen, shipbuilders, and warriors. They and their property were protected by the law, and they had the right to bear arms and participate in the ting. Some freemen were wealthier than others, and they generally lived in longhouses of various sizes.

At the bottom of society were the slaves. They were considered the property of their masters, like cattle, and they had no legal status or rights. A slave's master could sell, lease, free, punish, beat, or even kill the slave without any legal consequences. If someone else killed or injured a slave, he would have to compensate the slave owner. A slave woman's child became the slave of her master. The slaves performed the hardest and dirtiest work, they wore simple clothing, and they lived in poor conditions, usually in dugout huts. A freed slave was a freeman, but for several generations he and his descendants had a lower social status and fewer legal rights than other freemen.

The following is a slightly shortened English version of the Song of Rig. It describes how Rig visited three very different households and how he became the father of the slaves, the free farmers, and the nobility, in that order.

A LONG TIME AGO, a strong, wise god named Rig walked down green country lanes. On the middle road he approached a sod hut. The door was ajar, so he entered and saw a fire burning in the fire pit. An old couple was sitting there, dressed in old-fashioned clothes. They were Great-grandfather Ai and Great-grandmother Edda. Rig knew what to do. He sat down between the couple. Edda served a meal of thin broth and heavy, thick bread full of bran.

After the meal, Rig was tired, and he laid down in the middle of the bed with the couple on either side of him. He stayed with them for three nights, and then he left and made his way down the road.

Nine months later Edda gave birth to a baby with black hair. She sprinkled the baby with water, and named him Thrall, which means slave. Thrall grew up and became strong. He had rough, wrinkled hands with gnarled knuckles, thick fingers, an ugly face, a crooked back, and big feet. He worked hard all day long binding rope, bundling loads, and carrying wood to the house for burning.

A crooked-legged girl named Thir (meaning slave woman) came into the yard. She had a hooked nose, sunburned forearms, and muddy soles. Thrall and Thir sat together in the house, talked, and went to bed. They raised many children with hideous names and were fairly happy. Their kids built fences around the yard, spread manure on the fields, fed the goats, tended the swine, and worked the soil. Their descendants were the class of slaves.

Rig walked down the high road, and came to another dwelling. The door was unlocked, so he entered and saw a fire burning in the hearth. A couple was sitting there, working intently. The man was carving wood for a loom. He had short brown hair, a nicely-trimmed beard, and a shirt bound with leather. There was wood planking on the floor. The woman stretched her arms and held the distaff, for she was making a dress. She wore a cap and a smock, a kerchief on her neck, and brooches at her shoulders. Their names were Grandfather Afi and Grandmother Amma, and they owned the house.

Rig knew what to do. He was tired and slept in the center of the bed between the couple. He stayed there for three nights, and then he walked down the road.

Nine months later Amma had a son. She bathed him, wrapped him in clean linen, and called him Karl, which means farmer. He had a ruddy complexion and squinty eyes. Karl grew up and thrived well. He learned how to timber the house, tame the steers, raise the barns, build carts, and turn the plow to make furrows in the soil.

They brought home a girl in a goatskin gown. She put on a bridal veil, and they wed her to Karl. Her name was Snör, which means daughter-in-law. Karl and Snör exchanged rings and made a home together. She kept the keys to the house and the chest of valuables. They laundered sheets and worked the farm. They also raised many children with good names, and were fairly happy. From their children is descended the class of farmers.

Rig continued farther down the high road. He came to a magnificent hall with wide doors facing south. The gate was closed, and there was a beautifully patterned wooden ring on the gatepost. Rig entered the hall and found rushes on the floor. A couple named Father and Mother were facing each other, working with their hands.

The husband sat on a stool, twisted bowstrings, bent a bow, and sharpened arrows. The housewife sat there; thinking of her arms, she straightened her sleeves. She was smoothing linen and folding hems. She wore a high headdress, finely decorated brooches, a blue blouse, and a long gown. Her brow was brighter, her breast fairer, her neck whiter than the whitest flour.

Rig knew what to do. He sat down between the couple in the center of the hall. Then Mother brought a patterned cloth of white linen and covered the table. She also brought thin loaves of white bread and laid them on the tablecloth. She set the table with silver dishes filled with herring and roast fowl, and tankards of wine poured into tall goblets. They drank and talked until dusk.

Rig rose and readied the bed, stayed there three nights, and then strode down the road. Nine months later Mother had a baby. She bathed him, wrapped him in silk clothes, and named him Jarl, which means earl. He had blond hair, bright cheeks, and piercing eyes like a young snake. Jarl grew up in the hall and learned how to bend bows, polish arrows, ride horses, run the hounds, swim the sounds, and wield lances and swords.

Rig returned through the woods to teach Jarl the secrets of the runes, called him Rig, and considered him to be his son. He urged him to conquer age-old halls.

So Jarl rode his horse through forests and over mountain passes until he came to a hall. He gathered a group of loyal followers, brandished his shield, shook his spear, spurred his horse, drew his sword, roused to battle, reddened the fields with blood, felled warriors, and conquered the land. Soon he ruled over eighteen estates. He shared his wealth, making gifts of gold, silver, sleek horses, and rings.

His messengers rode over wet roads to the hall of a chieftain who had a daughter named Erna. She was fair and wise with a slender figure. The messengers asked for her hand and took her home. She wore a bridal veil and became Jarl's bride. They bedded together, lived at peace and pleased themselves, raised many children with beautiful names, and enjoyed their lives. Jarl's offspring grew up there and broke horses, bent shields, shook their spears, and polished their arrow shafts. They also played sports and board games, and all could swim.

Jarl's youngest son Kon (the future king) learned the runes and their meanings. He knew how to help men, blunt swords, and still the seas. He could understand bird language. He healed wounds and quenched flames, and he had the strength and energy of eight men. Kon exchanged runes with Jarl and surpassed him in knowledge. That is how he earned the right to be called Rig, the rune-knower.

Kon rode through the dark forest and shot birds with his arrows. Then a crow on a branch said to him, "Why do you spend your time hunting birds? You should be out riding horses, wielding swords, and slaying an army. Two of your brothers already have impressive halls and greater wealth than you. They know well how to handle swords, to sail the seas, and to spill the blood of enemies."

# CHAPTER THREE:
# *Tales of Gods and Giants*

*3. Urnes stave church carving of Ragnarok,
photo by Nina Aldin Thune*

BEFORE THEY CONVERTED TO CHRISTIANITY in the 10th and 11th centuries, the Norwegians and other Scandinavians in Viking times had their own Norse religion. From the Viking age we can find some references to gods and giants in skaldic poems and in the journals of Christian missionaries who visited Scandinavia.

Further evidence of Norse beliefs has been uncovered by archeologists at Viking burial sites.

However, most of our information about Norse mythology is derived from Icelandic sagas that were written in the 13th century, more than a hundred years after the end of the Viking age. These sagas were written versions of oral histories, songs, and poems that had been handed down over several generations. While some experts believe that they are mostly reliable, others claim that they were tainted by Christian beliefs because they were recorded by Christian historians. In any event, the evidence from the sagas, the skaldic verses, and the archeological finds gives us a fairly good understanding of the belief system in pre-Christian Viking society in Norway.

The Norwegians apparently believed that the world was flat, and that it was surrounded by a great ocean and supported by a huge tree called Yggdrasil. The people lived in Midgard in the middle of the world. There were many gods who protected the people, and they were divided into two groups called the Aesir, who lived in Asgard, and the Vanir. Opposing the gods were the evil, dangerous giants who lived in Jotunheimen. The tail of the Midgard Serpent wrapped around the earth, and a gigantic, vicious wolf named Fenrir was chained to a rock in the earth's center.

The gods were envisioned to be in human form with manlike traits and feelings, but also possessing supernatural powers. The leader of the Aesir was Odin, the inscrutable god of war, wisdom, magic, and poetry. He only had one eye, having given up his other eye for a drink at the Well of Wisdom. Accompanied by his two ravens Hugin and Munin (meaning thought and memory), Odin rode his eight-legged horse Sleipnir across the sky and wielded his mighty spear Gungnir. Odin was the favorite god of kings, chieftains, and warriors, all of whom aspired to be like him. Before a battle, the Vikings made sacrifices to Odin because he determined in advance who would win the battle and who would die. One of the reasons that the Vikings were so fierce and courageous in battle was that they believed that their fate had been predetermined by Odin.

Odin's son Thor was the mightiest of the gods, and he defended Asgard from the giants. Thor combined strength and bravery, and he also determined the weather, including thunder and lightning, winds and rains. He rode a chariot pulled by goats across the heavens, and his favorite weapon was Mjøllnir, his powerful hammer. The Vikings could easily relate to him because he had the most human qualities of any of the gods. That is, he was down-to-earth, even gullible, with a bad temper and sometimes not too bright. Therefore, Thor was the favorite god of the common man, the farmer, who drank a toast to him and asked him for rain and good weather for his crops. Many farmers named their children and their farms after Thor. Viking women wore amulets and pendants of Thor's hammer.

Loki was a cunning, unreliable trickster who frequently caused trouble for both the gods and the giants. He was the son of a giant and a goddess, and the father of the Midgard Serpent and Fenrir the wolf. Loki would often come up with devious plots and schemes. He was envious of Balder, another son of Odin who was the handsome, wise, articulate favorite of all the other gods.

The principal Vanir gods were Njord, the god of seafaring and fishing, and his son and daughter Frey and Freya, the god and goddess of fertility. The Vikings gave offerings to Njord in advance of a voyage at sea, and to Frey and Freya at weddings.

The Norwegians worshipped their gods in their longhouses and also outdoors in groves and mountains. From time to time they would hold a ceremony called a *blot* in the hall of the chieftain. At this ceremony they sacrificed horses, oxen, goats, pigs, and rams, sprinkled the blood of the animals on the walls and idols, and cooked the sacrificed animals. Then the chieftain blessed the food, and everyone feasted and drank beer with toasts to Odin for victory, to Njord for safe voyages, to Frey for fertility, and to their ancestors. Sometimes they even sacrificed humans, as when the heathen Jarl of Lade, the ruler of Western Norway, had his own son killed as a sacrifice in order to win a great victory in a sea battle against the Danes in AD 986.

The gods and giants were the subjects of countless stories told by skalds and others at their feasts and celebrations. Three of the most popular stories were The Lay of Thrym, the death of Balder, and the final battle called Ragnarok.

## The Lay of Thrym

Thor woke up one morning and looked for his hammer, but it was nowhere to be found. The mighty god of thunder flew into a rage and tore his beard. Then he complained to Loki that someone must have stolen his hammer. They both went to visit Freya, and Loki borrowed her cloak of feathers and flew to the hall of the giants. There he saw Thrym, the king of the giants, who admitted with obvious pleasure that he had taken Thor's hammer and hidden it eight miles below the ground. He refused to give it back until Thor fetched Freya to be Thrym's new bride.

Loki flew back to the hall of the gods and informed Thor what had happened. He also assured Thor that for once he was not lying or up to some mischief. They hurried over to Freya, and Loki told her to put on a bridal veil so she could marry the king of the giants. Freya absolutely refused, and the goddess of love replied that she was not so desperate for a man that she would marry a giant.

Since Freya was uncooperative, the gods and goddesses assembled in the hall of judgment to figure out how to recover Thor's hammer. Heimdall, the wisest of the gods who could see the future, came up with a solution. He suggested that Thor dress up like a woman, wearing a bridal veil, Freya's necklace, a belt with hanging keys, a long dress to hide his legs, brooches at his breast, and a nice cap covering his red hair. Then he could go to Thrym, pretend he was Freya, and retrieve his hammer. Thor did not think much of Heimdall's idea. He did not want the gods to laugh at him and call him a woman. But Loki persuaded him that it was the only way to get the hammer back, and that without the hammer to protect Asgard, the home of the gods would be lost to the giants.

So they dressed Thor in woman's clothes, and Loki decided to accompany him as his bridesmaid on the journey to the hall of the giants. Thor summoned his goats and his chariot, and off they went.

Thrym eagerly awaited the arrival of his new bride, and he instructed the giants to prepare the hall for the wedding feast. That evening they served a large supply of ale and good food. Thor was ravenously hungry, and he wolfed down a whole ox, eight salmon, plus all the food that was set out for the women, and he drank over three horns of mead. Thrym was taken aback that his dainty bride could eat and drink so much with such huge mouthfuls. But Loki explained it away by telling Thrym that the bride had not eaten for eight days because she was so wild with longing for her wedding day.

Then Thrym lifted the bridal veil so he could kiss the bride, but he jumped back when he saw the fierce look of fire in the bride's eyes. Loki explained that the bride looked like that because she had not slept for eight long nights in anticipation of her wedding day. Thrym's arrogant sister asked for a dowry of red golden rings before she would give her blessing to the marriage. To honor the bride, Thrym told the giants to bring the hammer and set it on the bride's lap, and to wish them happiness.

When he saw his hammer, Thor laughed in his heart, snatched the hammer, struck Thrym to the ground, and then killed all of the giant's relatives. Instead of giving the sister a bridal gift, he gave her a blow to the head. And that is how Thor recovered his mighty hammer.

### The death of Balder

Balder, the handsome son of Odin and the favorite of all the gods except Loki, was having bad dreams about death. So his father rode his horse to the realm of the dead, where they were preparing for someone's arrival. Odin asked a seeress to explain Balder's dreams and to tell him the reason for the preparations. She reluctantly told Odin that they were getting ready for Balder's arrival because he would soon be killed by his brother, the blind god Hod.

Odin returned home and told his wife Frigg why their son was having nightmares. Frigg became alarmed because she did not want her beloved son to die. So she summoned all creatures and all other things, including fire, water, rocks, metals, trees, plants, poisons, and animals, and at her request they all swore that they would not harm Balder.

When the other gods found out that Balder could not be harmed, they started playing a game. They attacked Balder with arrows, spears, swords, axes, and rocks, but nothing could hurt him.

The evil trickster Loki was envious of Balder, and he made plans to have him killed. Loki disguised himself as an old woman and asked Frigg if there was anything that had not taken the oath not to harm Balder. Frigg replied that she had not asked the little mistletoe to swear because it was so young. Then Loki uprooted the mistletoe, made it into an arrow, and gave it to the blind god Hod so he could join in the game. He pointed Hod in the right direction, Hod shot the arrow, and Balder was dead.

The other gods were overcome with grief. They prepared Balder's body for the funeral pyre on his ship and set it afire. Then the gods captured Loki and chained him to three large rocks. Loki remained there until he finally escaped before the final battle of Ragnarok between the gods and the giants.

## Ragnarok

The gods know that Ragnorok is inevitable, and that they will all die in the battle. There are ominous portents such as years without summers, wars among families, earthquakes, and tidal waves. Wolves swallow the sun and the moon, and the stars fall from the sky. Loki slips out of his chains and joins the giants. The Midgard Serpent emerges from the great ocean. Fenrir the wolf breaks his chains and runs loose. They all advance toward Asgard. Heimdall blows his horn to alert the gods, and Odin forms his army of gods and slain Viking warriors.

As the battle begins to rage, Frey is cut down by a fire giant. Odin spears Fenrir, but the wolf devours him before being torn apart by Odin's son Vidar. Thor and the Midgard Serpent fight each other to the death, as do Loki and Heimdall. Then the earth is consumed in flames and engulfed by the ocean, and the gods and giants are all dead.

But after the great battle, a new world emerges from the sea. Balder comes back to life, and the children of the gods live to take their places. A man and woman survive to start a new human race and enter a golden age.

# CHAPTER FOUR:
# *The Lay of Harald Fairhair*

*4. Three swords monument at Hafrsfjord*

E ARLY IN THE AGE OF THE VIKINGS, Norway was divided into
many different regions, each ruled by a nobleman called a
petty king, jarl, or chieftain. A petty king named Harald
Fairhair (or Harald Luva) unified much of the country and became
the first King of Norway in the late ninth century. He accomplished
this feat by entering into alliances with other noblemen who were

willing to recognize him as their overlord, and by waging war against the kings and chieftains who did not support him. The wars culminated in the Battle of Hafrsfjord, a sea battle in a fjord near present-day Stavanger, where Harald's fleet won a decisive victory over the remaining rebels and completed the unification of the first Kingdom of Norway.

Harald kept many residences in southwestern Norway, and the king and his court would move from one residence to the next throughout the year. At each residence, it was the responsibility of the local farmers to provide the king's court with food, drink, and other supplies. The king's principal residence was at Avaldsnes, a strategic point along the shipping lane of Western Norway. Avaldsnes had already been the home of many kings and chieftains for centuries, and Harald probably confiscated it from one of the defeated rebel noblemen. From there Harald collected taxes, rents, and fines from his subjects, and he imposed tolls on the ships that passed by.

King Harald's court was comprised of his family, his closest companions, and a hird of professional warriors. He also employed court poets called skalds, as well as musicians and jesters, all of whom entertained everyone at banquets in his ceremonial halls. The skalds composed and sang or chanted poems, including verses that praised the king, his ancestry, and his mighty deeds.

One of Harald's favorite skalds was Torbjørn Hornklove, who wrote a poem called The Lay of Harald (*Haraldskvedet*). Since the poem was written during Harald's lifetime by a member of his retinue, it is deemed to be a reliable (if somewhat embellished) account of King Harald, the Battle of Hafrsfjord, and the king's court. The poem is reconstructed from two sources: *Fagrskinna*, an ancient work meaning beautiful parchment, and *Heimskringla*, a history of the kings of Norway by the Icelandic chieftain and chronologist Snorri Sturluson. Parts of the poem have been lost to history.

The story in the poem is presented through a dialog between a Valkyrie and a raven. In Norse mythology, the Valkyries were maidens who transported deceased Viking warriors to Valhalla,

Odin's hall of the slain, where they would feast and fight in preparation for Ragnarok, the final battle between the gods and the giants. The raven was a popular Viking symbol, a scavenger that feasted on the bodies of the fallen after a battle.

This is an English version of The Lay of Harald. After some of the verses, there are notes of explanation in brackets.

1 Listen, you ring-bearers, while I tell you of Harald, the mighty and wealthy, and his courageous exploits of war. I overheard these words spoken by a haughty, fair-haired Valkyrie maiden and a shiny-beaked raven.
[The skald is reciting the poem to members of King Harald's court. They wore neck rings, arm rings, and finger rings that they received as gifts from the king.]

2 The Valkyrie was wise and bright-eyed, but she had no time for lovers. She could understand the language of the birds. The plain-speaking, blond-lashed maiden was greeted by the raven as he was perched on a cliff; he whose flight cut through the sky that was formed of the giant Ymir's skull.
[In Norse mythology, Odin and his two brothers killed a frost giant named Ymir and used his body to create the earth. Ymir's skull formed the dome of the sky.]

3 She said to the raven: "Where have you ravens been, with your beaks all gory at the break of dawn? You reek of decaying flesh, and your claws are bloody. In the night, were you at a place where you knew that corpses were lying?"
[The ravens have just returned from a night of feeding on dead bodies after a battle.]

4 The dun-colored raven shook himself off and dried his beak. The brother of eagles gave his answer some thought and replied, "Since we

crept out of the egg, we have been following Harald, Halvdan's first-born, the young Yngling."

[Harald is described as a young member of the Yngling family. Before the Viking age, this noble family supposedly migrated from Old Uppsala in Sweden to Vestfold on the west side of the Oslofjord, where they established petty kingdoms. Harald was the first-born son of a petty king named Halvdan the Black.]

5 "You know, the king who lives at Kvinnar, the commander of hordes of Northmen, who owns hollow warships with reddish ribs and reddened war shields, with tarred oar blades, and with tents sprinkled with the foam of the sea."

[Harald had a residence at Kvinnar in Hordaland in Western Norway. He commanded a large army of Norwegians. Vikings typically placed their shields on the sides of their ships to protect them when they were rowing. The ships and the shields were reddened with blood stains from battle. The ships and oars were periodically coated with tar to preserve them. Tents were placed in the center of Viking ships to protect cargo, weapons, and sleeping rowers from the weather and the foam of the sea.]

6 "Gladly the warlord drank the ale and played Frey's game at Yuletide. Even as a boy he hated the coziness of the hearth fire, the warm room of the women, and their padded down pillows."

[Harald was a heathen who lived before Christianity was established in Norway, so he celebrated Yuletide as a pagan midwinter feast. Frey was the Norse god of fertility, so Frey's game may refer to Harald's dalliance with women. Some say that the second sentence of this verse means that Harald became a Viking warrior at an early age. Clearly he was a Viking ruler who relished combat.]

7 "Have you heard how the highborn king fought there at Hafrsfjord against Kjotve the Rich? The enemy fleet came from the east, eager for battle, with gaping figureheads and richly carved bows."

[Harald's main opponent at the Battle of Hafrsfjord was a petty king named Kjotve, whose name means fat. Kjotve's fleet sailed to Hafrsfjord from the east, so presumably that part of Norway called Agder was not conquered by Harald until this battle. Viking ships often had figureheads of dragons or serpents on their beautifully carved bows.]

8 "The ships were full of farmer-warriors and gleaming shields, spears from the Westlands, and Frankish swords. As the battle was about to rage, the frenzied berserkers roared, the wolf-coated warriors howled and shook their weapons."

[Many of the rebel warriors were free farmers who were the subjects of the rebel chieftains. Westlands means the British Isles (perhaps Ireland or Scotland), and Frankish swords were considered the strongest and best. The berserkers, also called wolf-coats, were fierce warriors who screamed as they charged into battle with no apparent concern for their personal safety.]

9 "They taunted the great king of the Eastmen who lives at Utstein, but he forced them to flee. When the battle started, he steered out his ships, the steeds of Nokkvi. Blows were struck on shields before Haklang was fallen."

[Eastmen was a British term for Norwegian Vikings (men from the east of the British Isles), so the first sentence refers to Harald as the king of the Norwegians. Harald also had a residence at Utstein, not far from Avaldsnes. His ships are compared to the horses of a sea king named Nokkvi. The rebel named Haklang (meaning long man with a hairlip), who was killed in the battle, may have been Kjotve's son. Some claim that Haklang was Olav the White, the Viking King of Dublin, who left Ireland and returned home to Norway so he could fight alongside his family.]

10 "Weary of defending the land of his fathers from Luva, the bull-necked nobleman Kjotve took shelter behind an island. Those who

were wounded lowered their heads downward toward the keels of their ships. They hid under benches with their buttocks stuck up in the air." [Luva was another name for Harald. It means tanglehair (messy, unkempt hair), so it seems to confirm the legend that Harald refused to cut or comb his hair until he conquered all of Norway. Then one of his jarls cut his hair, and thereafter he was called Harald Fairhair. When the battle was lost, the wounded rebels tried to hide under their rowing benches.]

11 "The fleeing men held the shields of Gladhome on their backs as they were showered with stones. They struggled home from Hafrsfjord and fled over Jæren, thinking of their horns of mead." [Gladhome was the mythical home of Odin, and its roof was made of shields. As the rebels fled, they placed their shields on their backs because Harald's men were slinging rocks at them. The rebels looked forward to drinking mead when they got home instead of continuing to fight against Harald.]

12 "On the gravel lay the slain, given to Odin the one-eyed husband of Frigg. We, the ravens, were glad of such doings." [The fallen warriors were to be taken to Valhalla. The ravens were glad because their scavenging could begin.]

13 "The haughty maids of Ragnhild now have to babble of things other than Harald not feeding the fallen to the wolves, as their friends had often done." [Ragnhild was the Danish noblewoman who becomes Harald's consort in verse 14. Her maids had apparently said that Harald was not aggressive enough in battle. But he proved them wrong, so then they had to gossip about something else.]

14 "The noble lord took the lady from Denmark, forsaking his mistresses from Rogaland and their sisters from Hordaland, Hedmark, and Hålogaland."

[Harald kept many women as wives or mistresses, and they came from all over Norway, even from the inland province of Hedmark that was not thought by some to have been part of Harald's kingdom. Hålogaland was Northern Norway. After the battle, Harald took Ragnhild, the lady from Denmark, as his principal companion.]

15 Valkyrie: "Will the king who hastens the battle be generous to those who faithfully drive his opponents from his homeland?"
[After successfully conquering all of Norway, King Harald rewarded his hird with treasures in order to keep their loyalty.]

16 Raven: "Yes, the gallant warriors who spend their spare time playing board games in Harald's hall are cheered that he rewards them with much wealth, strong swords, gold from the land of the Huns, and women from the east."
[Harald was obviously very generous. The Vikings liked to play board games and dice.]

17 "They are happiest and aroused when they are called to battle, and then they row so hard that they snap the thongs and break the tholepins. They churn the waves briskly at the bidding of their king."
[When the king called them to fight, the warriors were so eager and rowed so hard and fast that they broke the thongs and tholepins that secured the oars to the ships.]

18 Valkyrie: "Since you boast of your knowledge, I ask you how the skalds are treated. How do the bards fare in Harald's halls?"
[The bards were skalds.]

19 Raven: "As seen from their fine clothing and their red and gold finger rings, they have a kind king. They have finely-bordered red fur cloaks, swords wound with silver, mail shirts of rings, golden chest-belts, graven helmets, and heavy gold bracelets, all as gifts from Harald."

[In part of the second sentence, the raven seems to be describing the attire of warriors rather than skalds.]

20 Valkyrie: "What about the berserkers, I ask you, you who thrive on corpses? How do the fighters fare, those who rush forth to battle and stoutheartedly stand against the foe?"

21 Raven: "The brave warriors who carry bloody shields into battle are called wolf-coats. The darts redden when they dash into battle and stand shoulder to shoulder. It is only men tried and true, those who can shatter shields, whom the wise warlord wants in battle."
[The berserkers (wolf-coats) sometimes stood shoulder to shoulder in battle to fight together, to protect the king behind them, and to form a shield wall.]

22 Valkyrie: "I have not asked you much about Andath and the other jesters. How do the fiddlers and the jugglers fare in the halls of Harald?"

23 Raven: "Your friend Andath fondles his earless dog; the jester with his foolish tricks makes the king chuckle. And there are others who carry bowls of hot wine around the fire. They tuck their flapping fool-caps firmly in their belts. They are fellows you are free to kick."
[The jesters played silly tricks to entertain the king and his warriors. The fools secured their caps so that the warriors could not knock them off their heads or throw them around. The warriors sometimes kicked the jesters and made fun of them. One can imagine the scene of a great feast and celebration of King Harald Fairhair and his hird with much food and drink, songs, stories, and laughter.]

# CHAPTER FIVE:
# *St. Sunniva*

5. *Statue of St. Sunniva*

T HE 10TH AND EARLY 11TH CENTURIES IN NORWAY were a
time of transition from paganism to Christianity. Harald
Fairhair's son Håkon became the foster son of the King of
England and was raised as a Christian. When he became the King of
Norway in AD 934, he tried to convert the heathens in Norway to
Christianity with the assistance of an English bishop and priests, and
several churches were built along the west coast. In this effort, he was
opposed by many chieftains and farmers, especially in Trøndelag and

Northern Norway, and he even had to modify his Christian beliefs to maintain their loyalty. After Håkon's death in about AD 961, a Danish interregnum led to an increase in paganism under the rule of the Danish kings' regents, the Jarls of Lade.

But in the late 10th and early 11th centuries, Norway was ruled by Norwegian and Danish kings who were Christians, and the Christian religion was firmly established, first by King Olav Tryggvason (who ruled from AD 995 to 1000) and later by King Olav Haraldsson (ruling from AD 1016 to 1028 and subsequently canonized as St. Olav) and his English Bishop Grimkell. Olav Haraldsson founded the Church of Norway and required everyone in Norway to be baptized and to follow Christian rules of morality. As the leaders of the Christian church in Norway, the Christian kings used their religion not only to convert the people, but also to increase their own authority and to reduce the independence and power of the local chieftains.

An illustration of this transition from the Norse religion to Christianity is the story of a Christian princess from Ireland who moved to Norway and faced discrimination and death at the hands of the heathens. Her name was Sunniva.

SUNNIVA WAS A BEAUTIFUL VIRGIN, a Christian princess in Ireland in the 10th century. After the death of her father, her kingdom in Ireland was conquered by a heathen Viking chieftain who wanted to force her to marry him. Instead, she and her followers, including men, women, and children, fled in three ships out onto the ocean. They decided to leave themselves in God's care, so they did not use any navigation, sails, or oars. The winds and the currents took the ships across the North Sea to the west coast of Norway, but they were driven away from the shore by heathen Norwegians who attacked them with stones and arrows. So they fled in their ships back out to sea, where they were separated in a bad storm. Finally Sunniva's ship and another ship landed at an uninhabited island called Selja near the mouth of the Nordfjord. There they settled and lived a peaceful, austere, simple existence in mountain caves because they were afraid of attracting the attention of the heathen Norwegians who lived on the mainland. Their diet consisted of just fish, birds, and water.

The island was otherwise deserted except for some sheep that were grazing there. The sheep were owned by Norwegian farmers on the mainland. When some of the sheep went missing, the farmers suspected that the Christians had taken them for food. So the farmers asked the heathen Jarl Håkon of Lade, the ruler of Western Norway, to come to Selja with his army and kill the Christians. When Sunniva and her followers saw the heathen army approaching, they were afraid they would be ravaged and killed. So they hid in the mountain caves, and crying out they prayed to God to send his angels to crush the mountain and bury them so their souls could find eternal rest. Suddenly the caves collapsed, all of the Christians were killed, and the jarl and his men had to withdraw.

Sometime later, two heathen merchants on their way to Trondheim anchored their ship for the night at Selja. They witnessed a bright, supernatural light rising from the mountain to heaven. Their curiosity led them to the mountain where they discovered a white skull that had a wonderful fragrance. They took the skull to Trondheim, showed it to the new Christian King Olav Tryggvason, and told him what they had seen on the island. Some other witnesses reported the same story to the king.

So in 996 King Olav and Bishop Sigurd traveled to Selja along with other priests. They examined and excavated the site, and in the mountain rubble they found human remains with sweet smelling bones. They also discovered the unharmed body of Sunniva, who appeared to be asleep. Her body was placed in a shrine that was kept in a chapel that they built outside the entrance to one of the caves.

For hundreds of years thereafter, Christian pilgrims came from all over Norway and the rest of Europe to pray at the altar of the chapel and to drink the water from the spring in the cave, which was said to heal their infirmities. In the 12th century, Sunniva's shrine was moved to a new cathedral in Bergen. In the great Bergen fire of 1170, her shrine was temporarily removed and held up to stop the advance of the fire, which was considered a miracle. Her shrine was moved once again in 1531, this time to a local monastery that was destroyed in the Reformation in 1536.

Sunniva was never canonized by the pope, but she was considered the local saint of Western Norway. She was described as gentle and kind, but with the courage and determination to confront and reject the aggression of brutal men. A picture or statue of Sunniva holding a stone was found in many medieval churches in Norway, sometimes accompanied by an image of St. Olav. Her feast days of July 8 and either August 31 or September 7 are still celebrated by the Roman Catholic Church in Norway.

Sunniva's cave and the ruins of the chapel are visible on the island of Selja. The inside of the cave is narrow, but the entrance is tall and wide with a view over the sound. In windy weather, you can hear the roar of the ocean from inside the cave, so the cave is called Dønhelleren, which means the rumbling echo cave.

# CHAPTER SIX:
# The Downfall
# of St. Olav

*6. Nidaros Cathedral in Trondheim*

OLAV HARALDSSON, LATER CALLED ST. OLAV, was the King of Norway from 1016 to 1028. During his reign, he established a central administration over all of Norway including the inland areas that had not been controlled by his predecessors. He appointed *lendmenn* who administered various regions of Norway on his behalf.

However, there were continued conflicts between King Olav and some of the chieftains, who resented the king's authoritarian rule and wanted to retain their independence and authority in their local areas. While some chieftains had been appointed lendmenn, others were not, and all of them saw their powers diminished by the king. Moreover, Olav established the Church of Norway led by the king, and his determination to Christianize the country also brought him into conflict with the remaining pagan chieftains and farmers who resisted the new religion.

So Olav's tenure as king was characterized by relative peace and stability, but with an undercurrent of dissatisfaction by various powerful men. That was especially true in Northern Norway, where paganism and the Norse religion were not fully subdued, and where independent chieftains conducted their own affairs far from the king's center of power in Southern Norway. Any dissent was unacceptable to the king, who tried to maintain a strict rule and did not tolerate insubordination. Ultimately, this conflict led to the end of his reign and his death at the hands of rebel chieftains and farmers, as told in the following story.

IN THE EARLY 1020S, THERE WAS A FAMINE IN NORWAY, especially in the northern part of the country. For three years in a row, the grain crop failed, and many people did not have enough to eat. For the northerners, the problem was compounded by the policies of King Olav, who tried to save the remaining stores of grain in the south by prohibiting anyone in Southern Norway from selling or delivering grain, flour, or malt up north. Malt was a valuable commodity that was used to make mead, the favorite drink of the Norwegians.

Asbjørn Sigurdsson was a young chieftain at Trondenes in Northern Norway. He was also the nephew of a powerful northern chieftain named Tore Hund (meaning Tore the Dog), who lived at Bjarkøy in Troms. For several generations, Asbjørn's family had hosted three heathen feasts each year, where family, friends, and followers would consume large quantities of food and drink for days on end. Asbjørn wanted to continue this tradition even though the feasts were frowned upon by the Christian king. But Asbjørn's once substantial stores of grain and malt were running low. To solve that problem, Asbjørn decided to travel south to obtain more grain and malt.

In the summer, he left on his voyage with 25 men on his well-equipped cargo ship with an impressive colored and striped sail. Many days later they arrived at Avaldsnes near present-day Stavanger. Avaldsnes was one of the king's finest estates, and it was managed by Tore Sel, a former slave who, through hard work, had risen in life to become the king's steward at that location. Despite his humble background, Tore Sel was an arrogant braggart who was known to recklessly run off at the mouth.

The morning after Asbjørn arrived at Avaldsnes, Tore Sel and his men came down to the ship to ask the owner what he was doing there and where he was going. Asbjørn explained that he wanted to buy grain and malt because they were suffering from famine in the north. Tore Sel replied that Asbjørn might as well turn his ship around and head back up north because the king had forbidden the sale of grain in the south. But Asbjørn replied that he also wanted to visit his uncle Erling Skjalgsson farther south at Sola, and he agreed to stop at Avaldsnes once again on his way home.

So Asbjørn and his men sailed to Sola, and they were well received by Erling. Asbjørn's Uncle Erling was one of the most powerful chieftains in all of Norway, and he commanded a large army and a fleet of ships. Asbjørn asked his uncle to sell him grain. But Erling explained to his nephew that it was a problem because the king had forbidden the sale of grain and Erling would have to obey the king's command.

However, the following day Erling came up with a solution to Asbjørn's problem. Erling said that his slaves would sell the grain to Asbjørn because they had no legal status and therefore they were not subject to the king's laws. Asbjørn bought grain and malt from the slaves, and set sail northward with a fully loaded ship. When he stopped at Avaldsnes, Tore Sel appeared with 60 men and confiscated all of the grain and malt. He was very nasty about it, and he even had his men remove the beautiful sail from Asbjørn's ship and replace it with an old sail, explaining that the old sail should work just fine to sail an empty ship. Asbjørn sailed empty-handed back home to Northern Norway, where people began to gossip about how Asbjørn had been humiliated by a former slave.

That winter, Asbjørn was not able to hold a feast, but Tore Hund invited Asbjørn and his mother Sigrid and their friends to his banquet. Tore Hund made fun of Asbjørn for submitting to a slave. Asbjørn was angry, and he decided to avenge the treatment he had received in the south. So the following spring, Asbjørn equipped a longship, set sail with a larger force of 90 men, and headed south. When they reached Avaldsnes, Asbjørn set off alone toward the king's estate. It was Easter week, and Asbjørn found out that King Olav was there to celebrate the religious holiday along with many of his subjects.

Asbjørn went to the king's hall where the king was eating dinner in his high seat at a banquet. Asbjørn waited in the entry room and heard Tore Sel bragging about how he had confiscated all of Asbjørn's grain, and that he had made Asbjørn cry by stealing his sail. At that point, an angry Asbjørn ran into the room, drew his sword, and cut off Tore Sel's head, which landed with a thud on the table right in front of King Olav.

The king was outraged that Asbjørn had murdered his steward and desecrated the Easter holiday. Asbjørn was arrested and placed in chains. His cousin Skjalg, Erling's son, happened to be at the banquet, and he approached the king and offered to pay a substantial fine to save Asbjørn from execution. The king refused, and Skjalg and his men left and rowed their boat as fast as they could to Sola, where they told Erling what had happened.

Erling immediately assembled a huge army of 1,500 men and set sail for Avaldsnes, determined to free his kinsman Asbjørn. They arrived on Sunday morning when the king was attending mass at the church, and they freed Asbjørn and removed his chains. After the mass, King Olav left the church, only to find Erling and his large army facing him. Erling bowed to the king, apologized for what Asbjørn had done, and offered to pay any fine that the king determined as long as Asbjørn would be pardoned and not banished from Norway. The king saw that he and his men were outnumbered by Erling's army, so he agreed to Erling's proposal. Olav even offered to appoint Asbjørn as his new steward in place of Tore Sel. But Asbjørn had no intention of becoming the king's slave in a position formerly held by a scoundrel like Tore Sel. So Asbjørn sailed back to Northern Norway, and from then on he was called Asbjørn Selsbane, meaning the person who slew Tore Sel.

After this tense confrontation, there was great enmity between Erling Skjalgsson and King Olav, and Olav alienated the northern chieftains by appointing a new lendmann named Åsmund Grankjelsson to rule half of Northern Norway on his behalf in place of a prominent northern chieftain. Furthermore, Olav revoked Asbjørn's pardon, and he sent Åsmund north to arrest and execute Asbjørn. Åsmund's fleet encountered Asbjørn at the rudder of his cargo ship in a narrow strait, and Åsmund murdered Asbjørn by throwing a spear that hit him right in the chest.

After Asbjørn's body was taken home to Trondenes, Asbjørn's distraught mother Sigrid sent word to Tore Hund, who arrived and officiated at the funeral. When Tore Hund was about to return home to Bjarkøy, Sigrid presented him with gifts, including the spear that had killed her son. She told him: "Here is the spear that went through Asbjørn, my son, and his blood is still on it. That makes it easier for you to remember what you should do with it. If you are a decent man, then stick the spear in the breast of King Olav. And this I tell you, that you will be considered a coward by everyone if you do not avenge Asbjørn's death." Tore Hund was angry, but he realized that he would have to kill the king.

Now there was an uprising against the king by chieftains in Southern and Northern Norway, and the rebels were supported by Knut the Great, the King of Denmark and England, who felt that he was the rightful King of Norway. The rebellion grew after King Olav's men captured Erling Skjalgsson in a sea battle, and one of the king's men killed Erling after the king had given him quarter. King Olav told the killer, "Now you have struck Norway out of my hands." He was right. People throughout Norway abandoned the king. Knut the Great invaded Norway and was proclaimed King of Norway in 1028, and Olav fled to the Viking kingdom in Russia.

In 1030 Olav returned to Norway with a small army and tried to retake his throne. On July 29, 1030, they faced a much larger army of farmers and chieftains at the Battle of Stiklestad north of Trondheim. At the beginning of the battle, Tore Hund led the charge of the farmers against Olav by yelling, "Forward, forward, you farmers!" And Olav and his men responded with "Forward, forward, you men of Christ, men of the cross, men of the king!" The battle was a bloody affair, and many men on both sides were cut down. King Olav fought bravely, but he was killed by three blows, including a thrust by Tore Hund of the same spear that had killed Asbjørn.

So Tore Hund avenged the death of his nephew. Olav Haraldsson was later declared a saint, and the great Nidaros Cathedral in Trondheim was built in his honor. Olav's half brother Harald Hardråde (meaning the hard ruler), who fought with him at Stiklestad, subsequently became the last Viking King of Norway. By the end of his reign in 1066, Harald had destroyed the power of the chieftains once and for all, and the Christian religion was firmly established in Norway.

# CHAPTER SEVEN:
# *The King's Mirror*

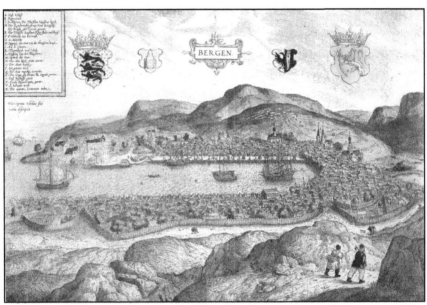

*7. Ancient drawing of Bergen*

T HE *KING'S MIRROR* (*KONGESPEILET*) is the most significant piece of medieval literature from Norway. It was written in the Old Norwegian language, probably in the 1250s during the reign of King Håkon Håkonsson, who had already ruled Norway for several decades since 1217. The period of Håkon's reign and that of his son and grandsons is called the Age of Greatness or the Golden Age because it was a time of relative peace, stability, and prosperity in Norway.

The author of *The King's Mirror* was apparently a high-ranking member of the king's court who may have lived in or near Trondheim. Some experts claim that he wrote this work as a book of instruction for the king's son, Prince Magnus, who subsequently ruled Norway from 1263 to 1280. As king, he was called Magnus the Lawmender because he and his advisors codified the laws of Norway. *The King's Mirror* provided the young prince with valuable information on the ways of the world and how to act in different situations. It contains scientific theories, a summary of world geography, and a description of the occupations of merchants and members of the king's court. It was also intended to describe the occupations of priests and farmers, but those sections are missing and were probably never written before the author died.

The information in *The King's Mirror* is presented in a dialog between father and son, both of whom are clearly members of Norway's upper class. The son has grown to adulthood and is ready to embark on a career, first to travel abroad as a merchant, and then to return home to join the king's entourage. At the son's request, his father gives him information and advice on those two occupations. So *The King's Mirror* provides a unique look at the lives of merchants and kingsmen in thirteenth century Norway.

The father describes a merchant as a well-to-do man who travels on his own ship to foreign lands, where he purchases, sells, and trades goods. The father's advice to the son includes the following:

- Do not defraud or steal from others, but always be honest, polite, friendly, and agreeable.
- Wear nice clothes and eat good food.
- In a foreign market town, find lodgings from the most discreet and popular innkeeper. Get up early, go to mass, then transact your business like the most prominent merchants in the town, have breakfast and lunch on nice table settings, take a nap, and then conduct more business.

- Examine goods before you buy them, and make your deals in front of witnesses.
- Set a fair price for the goods you are selling, and do not hold inventory too long if you can sell the goods at reasonable prices.
- Do not conceal any defects in your goods from the buyers.
- Study commercial law so you know the rules that apply to merchants and their transactions.
- Learn the customs and languages of the places where you conduct business, especially the Latin and French languages, and remain fluent in Norwegian.
- Hold your temper, but don't be a coward. Watch what you say, and do not speak in anger or use profanity, tattling, or slander. Avoid drunkenness, chess, prostitutes, and gambling.
- Pay all taxes and fees promptly, and maintain a good relationship with the local authorities.
- Only buy good ships, keep your ship attractive and in good shape, keep it well equipped, and travel only in the summer.
- Do not employ unruly men.
- If you accumulate capital, divide it into three parts. Invest one-third in partnerships with trustworthy, experienced businessmen who live in market towns. Invest the other two-thirds in other businesses. If you diversify your investments, you will not lose everything from one bad investment.
- If your investments turn out to be extremely profitable, draw out two-thirds and purchase good farmland, which is the most secure investment. Keep the remaining third in business, or use it to buy more land.
- When you become wealthy, discontinue your journeys and trading activities in foreign lands.

It is striking how at least some of this advice from medieval Norway could also be useful in modern times. When *The King's Mirror* was written, the days of wealthy, traveling Norwegian merchants were already numbered, as the Hanseatic merchants from the Baltic cities of

Northern Germany soon came to dominate the import-export trade in Norway and the rest of Northern Europe for centuries.

The author of *The King's Mirror* goes on to describe the court of the King of Norway as a very formal place with strict rules of etiquette. The composition of the court also reflected the king's concern for his own safety at a time not long after Norway's hundred years of civil wars (from 1134 to 1240), when pretenders to the throne and their armies sought to depose the kings by force. The father describes the following occupations in the king's retinue, and labels all those who serve as kingsmen.

- The lowest ranking men are attendants who do various jobs, including manual labor, at the king's residence or elsewhere under the direction of the king's steward.
- The gests are the king's spies who track down and kill his enemies throughout the kingdom. When a gest kills an opponent of the king, the gest may confiscate and keep the opponent's property, except for gold which goes to the king. At court, the gests do not dine with the king and the hird except at Christmas and Easter.
- There are farmers, merchants, and others who live away from the king's residence, but they are sometimes called upon to provide services to the king or his retinue.
- There are noblemen, merchants, bishops, clerks, and wealthy farmers who serve the king in other lands and on the seas as ambassadors, captains of the king's longships, and traders of the king's goods.
- The members of the hird are bodyguards who protect the king and always dine with him.
- The king's best men are his advisors such as the archbishop, bishops, various noblemen, and some members of the hird.

The father, who has a lot of experience as a former official of the king, also gives advice to his son on how to become part of the king's hird and how to act there.

- Get to know one of the king's favorites who will arrange an audience with the king. Appear at the king's hall dressed in your finest clothes and with your hair and beard trimmed and combed in the style of the court, accompanied by the kingsmen who support you.
- When you appear before the king, do not wear a hat, gloves, or a cloak. The kingsmen would think that you are trying to show up the king with fancy clothes or to act as the king's equal, or they might fear that you are hiding weapons in your clothing and that you intend to attack the king. Make sure you have bathed, and stand erect and dignified. Give the king his space, and address him politely at all times.
- After you are accepted into the hird, whenever you are in the presence of the king, do not converse with others, but always listen to the king.
- If the king speaks to you, and you do not hear or understand him, don't just say "Huh?" or "What?" Instead, politely ask the king to repeat what he said. But pay attention to the king, and don't ask him to repeat very often.

These are just a few of the many rules of conduct and other topics discussed in *The King's Mirror*. The book was undoubtedly helpful to Prince Magnus. During his subsequent reign as king, he increased the size and importance of the king's court by appointing a king's council to advise him on matters of state and by creating positions such as chancellor to play significant roles in the king's governance of the Kingdom of Norway.

# CHAPTER EIGHT:
# *The Maid of Norway*

*8. Håkonshallen – the hall of kings in Bergen*

I N MARCH OF THE YEAR 1286, King Alexander of Scotland enjoyed an all-day banquet with Scottish lords at Edinburgh Castle. By the evening he was intoxicated. Nevertheless, he decided to mount his horse and take a long ride to visit his beloved new wife. His aides advised him not to go because of his condition and an incoming storm. But the king insisted, so they sent two guides to accompany and safeguard the king. They rode to the ferry landing, where the ferryman at first refused to take them across the

Firth of Forth in the midst of a storm. The king ordered him to do so, and somehow they made it over the rough seas. But then back on land the king was separated from his guides, and he rode his horse right off a rocky embankment into the ocean, broke his neck, and drowned. The next day his body was found washed up on the shore. He was the last king of a family dynasty that had ruled Scotland for over 250 years.

Alexander's children had all preceded him in death, and the only remaining member of his family was young Princess Margrete in Bergen, Norway, Alexander's three-year old granddaughter and the only child of King Eirik of Norway. This little maiden became the Queen of Scotland, although that country was actually ruled by Scottish noblemen for the time being. She also became a pawn in a game of diplomatic intrigue that followed.

King Edward I of England laid claim to the throne of Scotland, and now he saw his chance to take over undisputed rule of that country. He sent diplomats to Bergen to ask King Eirik for the hand of the young princess for his son Prince Edward, the future King of England, and they offered Eirik a substantial sum of money plus English political support in Scandinavia.

In 1290, after four long years of negotiations between England, Scotland, and Norway, the three parties reached an agreement that the young maid of Norway would marry the Prince of England. A delighted King Edward sent a beautifully decorated ship to Bergen to pick up the princess and take her to England for the wedding. But the Scottish lords objected; they wanted her to go to Scotland to hold the wedding there. There were more negotiations that dragged on until the fall of the year, when all parties finally agreed to send the princess to Orkney, an island north of Scotland that was controlled by Norway's king. The plan was to sign a final marriage contract there, and then send her to Edinburgh for the wedding.

So in late September 1290 a large crowd of Norwegians gathered in Bergen to watch a grand procession, as the Princess of Norway and Queen of Scotland, seven-year old Margrete, walked from the king's fortress to the English ship, accompanied by Norwegian nobles and the Bishop of Bergen who would take her to Orkney. The ship contained large quantities of the best food and drink provided by the English king.

Unfortunately, the negotiations had taken so long that it was almost October, and the ship had to sail after the normal sailing season. Shortly after leaving Bergen, the ship encountered cold weather, storms, and very rough seas. Young Margrete became deathly ill from seasickness, and by the time they reached Orkney she was barely alive. They laid her in bed at the bishop's fortress at Kirkwall, Orkney, and tried to save her life. But she was too far gone. The bishop gave her the last rites, and she died in his arms.

Now she was dead, Edward's plans to take over Scotland peacefully were ruined, the Scottish royal dynasty was terminated, and the Scottish lords assembled an army and prepared for an expected war against England. In fact, Edward and his English army invaded Scotland in 1296, and the two countries fought against each other for years, as portrayed in the movie *Braveheart*. Eventually, after 30 years of war, the Scots prevailed, and Robert Bruce, an ally of the Norwegian kings, became the King of Scotland.

In the meantime, back in 1290, the English ship brought the body of young Margrete in her coffin back to Norway. A distraught King Eirik identified her body, and she was buried next to her Scottish mother at Christ Church in Bergen. The King of Norway had lost his only child and heir. In Scotland, the maid of Norway was never forgotten; she was memorialized for many years in song and poetic verse. But that was not the end of the story.

Shortly after Margrete was buried in Bergen, there were rumors in both Norway and Scotland that she was still alive. These rumors captured the imagination of many Norwegians. Their suspicions grew when King Eirik died in 1299, and his brother Håkon, the new king, suddenly had the highest ranking royal advisor, Audun Hugleiksson, arrested and thrown into a dungeon. Later he was beheaded without any explanation. Was it because he had something to do with the death or mysterious disappearance of the little princess? The Norwegians also suspected Ingeborg Erlingsdatter, the noblewoman who had accompanied Margrete to Orkney. She was from a family of Baltic pirates, and many Norwegians felt that she was up to no good.

Then in 1300, a German woman and her husband stepped off a ship in Bergen. She went around town claiming that she was the real Margrete, and that she had returned to Norway to rejoin the royal family. Her story was that Ingeborg Erlingsdatter had betrayed her and sold her into slavery for a large sum of money, but that on the way to Africa her captors had been intercepted by pirates who took her to Germany where she grew up. She said that the conspirators killed another girl and put her in the coffin, and that King Eirik was so devastated that he identified the wrong girl who was then buried.

This German woman spoke perfect Norwegian, and her story sounded credible. However, the problem was that she appeared to be about 40 years old and she had graying hair, whereas the real Margrete, if she had lived, would still have been a teenager. Nevertheless, many Norwegians, including commoners and priests, believed every word of her story, which confirmed their earlier suspicions.

However, the royal authorities called her an impostor. They arrested her and her husband and threw them into prison in Bergen, where they languished for several months until King Håkon returned from Oslo. When the king got back to Bergen, he agreed with his advisors, and the false Margrete and her husband were sentenced to death.

So in the fall of 1301 there was another large crowd of Norwegians who witnessed another procession. This time it was the condemned woman and her husband who walked from the fortress to the dock. When she emerged from the fortress, the woman reminded everyone in a loud voice that she was taking the same walk as she had done 11 years before, and then the crowd became even more convinced that she was the real Margrete. The waiting ship took the couple across the harbor to Nordnes, where she was burned at the stake and her husband was beheaded.

Even after the death of the false Margrete, the rumors and stories continued. Many considered her to be a holy martyr who could heal the sick, and more and more Norwegians made pilgrimages to the site of her execution, where a small church was built in her honor later in the 14th century. The cult of Margrete lasted until the Reformation in the 1500s. In the Faeroe Islands there is a ballad that tells the story of the maid of Norway who was betrayed by Norwegian nobles and later executed.

# CHAPTER NINE:

# A Legend of
# the Black Death

*9. Hedalen stave church in Valdres*

IN 1349 THE BUBONIC PLAGUE, also called the Black Death (*Svartedauen*), came to Norway. Over one-half of the population died. In some valleys, everyone succumbed to the disease and all the farms were abandoned for hundreds of years.

More than 200 years after the Black Death, a hunter was walking through an evergreen forest in Valdres. He shot an arrow that missed a bird, and after a few seconds he heard the distant ringing of a bell. He was curious, so he followed the sound of the bell and found an old church that was abandoned when everyone in the valley died of the plague. The door was open, and he walked inside where he was in for a big surprise.

This is an English translation of a legend of the Black Death called "The Ancient Church", as told by the famous Norwegian artist Theodor Kittelsen in his collection of stories and illustrations called *Svartedauen*, published in 1900.

A HUNTER WALKS ALONE through the deserted wilderness. Trees that are a hundred years old or more raise their giant trunks toward the sky, with their large dark branches loaded down with heavy snow. In the woods it is dark and silent, like a home for ugly trolls. There is only the sound of twigs that break when a moose makes his way through the underbrush. The hunter catches a glimpse of the northern lights as heavy snow falls through the tightly grown branches, blown by the cold breeze.

As he stops to listen, he hears a bird flapping its wings up in a tall evergreen tree. The hunter looks up, and very high in the tree a mighty grouse is proudly ruffling its feathers. And the hunter aims his bow – the arrow whistles through the trees, and haughtily the untouched bird flies away. But then in the dark forest the hunter hears the strangest ringing sound coming from where his arrow has disappeared. Like a dirge or a lament, a bell chimes in the stillness, as if the arrow has pierced the heart of the quiet solitude. The hunter cannot believe his ears.

As a shiver runs down his spine, he tries to figure out where the ringing sound came from, and he trudges through the heavy brush and bushes. He makes out something large and dark-colored, and he's shocked to see a tower, a roof, and a wide building. Between the trunks of pine trees there lies an old, hidden church, its roof partly collapsed, totally abandoned in the solitude of nature.

To save the old church from the devil, the superstitious hunter quickly grabs his flint and steel, and throws them over the building.

The church door with a rusty key in the lock is half open, and it looks dark and musty inside. Snow has blown in onto the floor, and it crunches under the hunter's shoes as he walks in and makes uneven tracks in the soft, white clumps of snow. In the middle of the floor there's a large bell that has fallen from the roof. Several more bells are hanging up there. One of them must have rung when it was struck by the arrow. All around in every corner where faint light shines through the openings in the roof, there are long icicles hanging down. They blink like diamonds in the dark old church, forgotten in humble solitude.

But wait! He hears the sound of breathing. Over there in front of the altar, something black and wooly is lying. The hunter approaches carefully. It's a big bear! The king of the forest is soundly asleep at the foot of the altar. Smacking his lips, his paws safely on his breast, the bear is dreaming in his winter hibernation.

The bear is having pleasant dreams of being king of the forest, king in the quiet stillness where countless branches cling together on the mountain ridge, shaggy and plump, just like the bear. The outline of tall, majestic mountains appears in the sunlight over the old bear's kingdom, and in the valley there are bogs and ponds, steaming full of adventure. Soon the spring will brighten the meadows, blue flowers spreading everywhere, evergreens, tempting bees' nests, and strawberries, cloudberries, blueberries, crowberries, cranberries, full patches of lingonberries. Think of wallowing in the marsh, then kill a moose and _____! The hunter's arrow pierces the bear's chest.

Gone are all the beautiful dreams. The bear strains to get up on two paws. Blood flows all around the altar. Lying against the altar board, he hugs his breast with the arrow that awoke him to die. And with a loud roar so the whole church shudders, he collapses to the floor.

The hunter skins the bear, and nails the hide to the church wall as a reminder of his ordeal.

For many, many years thereafter, the old remains of the bearskin hang on the church wall, a reminder of the hunter and the time when a bear sought refuge at the altar of the Lord.

Remember the past, while time quickly rushes on, and the memories become so dark and so strange, the ragged sacrifice of a bear's hide.


HEDALEN STAVE CHURCH IN VALDRES was rediscovered in 1558 by a hunter who killed a bear, after the church had been vacant and covered by forest since the Black Death. The church was just as the deceased priest and congregation had left it over 200 years before. The bearskin still hangs in the church vestry.

# CHAPTER TEN:

# *The Last Priest of Telemark*

*10. St. Michael's mountain on Norsjø*

AFTER THE NORWEGIAN POPULATION WAS DECIMATED by the Black Death, the kingdom's Golden Age was definitely over. Norway became a much weaker, poorer country that was ruled by Denmark for over 400 years from 1380 to 1814.

In 1536, in the midst of the Protestant Reformation in Europe, the new Danish king, a Lutheran known as Christian 3, issued a coronation charter in which he declared that Norway would forever after be considered just a province of Denmark. Furthermore, even though the vast majority of Norwegians at that time were devout Roman Catholics, within a year King Christian abolished the Catholic Church in Norway, arrested the Catholic bishops, expropriated all property of the Catholic Church, and established the Lutheran Church as the sole religious institution in Norway with himself as the leader of the church. The Archbishop of Norway, who was the last Norwegian with a leadership role in the country, fled to exile in the Netherlands in 1537 and died shortly thereafter. So Norway's Reformation was imposed by the Danish crown against the will of the Norwegian people.

At first the changes to the local churches in Norway were gradual. The Catholic churches became Lutheran churches, and the existing priests continued to serve their parishes. But over time the transformation picked up speed, as the imprisoned Catholic bishops were replaced by Lutheran superintendents, Catholic priests were fired or died, and Danish Lutheran pastors took over their parishes. Crucifixes and images of saints were removed from the churches, new Danish Bibles and hymnals were introduced, and a Danish worship service supplanted the Catholic Latin mass. Catholicism in any form was no longer tolerated by the Danish authorities in Norway.

As early as the 1300s, a small Catholic chapel had been built in a cave in the province of Telemark. Called St. Michael's Church, it was located about 30 meters up a rocky cliff on the east side of a large lake called Norsjø. Since the chapel was built, masses were held there on Catholic holy days such as St. Michael's Day on September 29 each year. A Catholic priest was assigned to the chapel, and he lived at the Gisholt farm not far away. There was also a Catholic cemetery at the top of the cliff, and in fact the place had been a center of religious activity since the age of the Vikings.

During the Reformation in Norway, the Lutheran authorities removed the Catholic priest from St. Michael's Church, and masses in the chapel were no longer permitted. But many of the farmers of

Telemark preserved their Catholic beliefs, and they disliked the new ways of the Lutheran Church. They also resented the closure of their beloved chapel at Norsjø, and Catholic pilgrims continued to visit the site to pray.

In the late 1500s a Danish Lutheran pastor named Povel Ringkøping became the Lutheran pastor in the Solum parish that included the area around Norsjø. Povel was a strict, stern, impatient man who was determined to remove the last remaining vestiges of Roman Catholicism from his parish once and for all.

On a dark autumn night, Povel was sitting in a boat on the lake while three oarsmen were ferrying him back to his parsonage. When the boat passed the cave, the oarsmen suddenly stopped rowing. They fell to their knees, crossed themselves, and said prayers. Povel was outraged at this display of the old religion. He looked up and saw a light emanating from the cave, and he could hear the faint sound of someone singing. He immediately ordered the men to row towards the cave, but instead they rowed in the opposite direction. They were afraid, and they thought that ghosts were worshipping in the cave. Povel became even more irate, and he vowed to return and find out what was going on in the cave. But none of the other local men were willing to take him there.

So he had to hire men from the city of Skien to bring their boat to the lake and row to the cave. On the night before St. Michael's Day, they rowed across the lake and let Povel off on the shore beneath the cave. It was a clear, still night, and once again a light from the cave was visible and singing could be heard. Povel wanted the oarsmen to go with him up to the cave, but they refused because they were afraid of the light and what they might find in the cave. Povel called them cowards and started climbing the steep path that led to the cave. As he approached the cave, he recognized the singing as part of a Catholic mass. But when he reached the mouth of the cave, the light from the cave disappeared and the singing stopped. Everything was dark and quiet.

At that point, Povel became somewhat apprehensive himself, not knowing what he might encounter in the cave. He had brought along his Danish Bible and his sword. So, trying to be brave, he drew the sword, clutched his Bible next to his chest, and walked into the cave singing Luther's Reformation battle hymn: "A mighty fortress is our God; a sword and shield victorious!" Before he could finish the first verse, the light reappeared, and he could see a small room at the back of the cave with many lit candles on an altar in front of a picture of a crucifix.

A bent-over old man emerged from the small room. He was dressed in the robes of a Catholic priest. The sight of the old priest was disarming to Povel, and he was ashamed that he was holding the sword. The pastor asked the priest who he was and what he was doing there, and he said that he could not tolerate the singing of a Catholic mass in his parish.

The old man invited the pastor into the small sacristy where he lived and prayed. He identified himself as Father Sylvester, and he told Povel his life story. He was the last ordained priest of St. Michael's Church. At the time of the Reformation, the Lutheran authorities forcibly removed him from his chapel. Since then, for several decades he had wandered as a pilgrim in foreign lands. But he decided to return to his chapel in his native Norway to die and be buried there. Sylvester assured Povel that pilgrims only came to the cave in the daytime, and that he had no contact with them because he stayed in his small sacristy that was closed off with a large stone. He only moved the stone away and sang his mass during the night. Therefore, he asked if he could just be left in peace for the short period of time until his death.

Povel was deeply moved by Father Sylvester's story, and he promised not to bother him as long as he did not say mass for others. Sylvester agreed, and they held each other's hands. As Sylvester followed the pastor out of the cave, Povel asked him if he needed any food. The priest replied that the people at the Gisholt farm brought him what little he needed, and that they had also agreed to bury him in the sand floor of the little sacristy and seal the entrance to that room after his death. He asked Povel not to punish the farmers for helping him, and Povel agreed.

They said their good-byes, and Povel climbed back down the cliff to the boat and returned to his parsonage. He continued to travel across the lake from time to time, observing the light from the cave. But then one night the light was gone, and Povel knew that the last priesr of St. Michael's chapel had been laid to rest. After Povel's meeting with Father Sylvester, everyone noticed that he was a changed man. He was visibly kinder and more gentle and forgiving.

The cemetery at the top of the cliff was still in use in 1643, and pilgrims continued to visit the cave well into the 1800s.

# CHAPTER ELEVEN:
# *The Witches*
# *of Finnmark*

*11. Steilneset Memorial in Vardø*

IN THE MIDDLE AGES and for some time thereafter, many Norwegians and other Europeans were superstitious and believed that there were witches and other beings who had supernatural powers. In medieval society, the people had no explanation for natural disasters or other problems, so they blamed them on witches, trolls, or monsters.

There were evil witches and good witches. The evil witches made a pact with the devil that gave them the power to inflict great harm. They cast spells and used black magic to cause sickness, infertility, injury, or death to people and livestock, to destroy crops, to create storms, fires, earthquakes, and avalanches, and to sink ships. The good witches used white magic and folk medicine and religion to help people by healing the sick or finding lost or stolen property. Some of the good witches were wandering, destitute women who offered to use their powers to do good deeds in exchange for money or food.

The superstitions were shared by priests and pastors. In fact, the Protestant Reformation unleashed tens of thousands of witch trials in Europe in the 16th and 17th centuries. Based on language in the Old Testament, Martin Luther believed that anyone who practiced witchcraft should be executed, whether it involved evil deeds or good deeds. Lutheran pastors considered witchcraft to be a false religion of devil worship, a renunciation of God and the Christian faith, and therefore a terrible sin. Although both men and women were accused of witchcraft, the pastors were especially suspicious of women as the successors of Eve, the woman in the Bible who made the first pact with the devil.

For several decades after the Norwegian Reformation in the 1530s, persecution of alleged witches and warlocks became widespread in Norway, and new criminal laws were enacted to punish anyone engaged in witchcraft. A new law in 1593 prescribed the death penalty for all witches, good or bad. This was modified by a decree in 1617 that continued the death penalty for evil witches, but changed the sentence for good witches to forfeiture of property and banishment from the country. Even people who were not witches themselves, but who asked good witches for help, were required by law to pay fines. The 1617 decree was issued to commemorate the 100th anniversary of the Lutheran Reformation in Europe.

These new laws became effective during the reign of Christian 4, the religious and superstitious King of Denmark and Norway from

1588 to 1648, who believed that there were witches and witchcraft. For example, in 1599 King Christian traveled with a Danish fleet to Northern Norway and the White Sea of Russia in order to assert the authority of Denmark-Norway in that region. On the way back to Denmark, off the coast of Northern Norway, they encountered a bad storm. Everyone started blaming a big black cat on board that the hornblower of the king's ship had stolen from a Sami woman in Russia. They figured that the Sami woman must have been a witch who was angry at them and cast a spell that caused the storm in order to sink the fleet. The pilot of the king's ship wanted to throw the cat overboard, but King Christian had grown attached to the cat and did not want it to drown. So instead, as ordered by the king, they placed the cat and enough food for a month in a washtub and cast the tub adrift in the ocean so it could take the cat back to the witch, who would then hopefully remove the spell and silence the storm. Strangely enough, after the cat was out of sight, the storm subsided and the fleet made it safely back home. In 1609 Christian sent a letter to the local authorities in Northern Norway, instructing them to execute any Sami who practiced witchcraft.

During the period from 1567 to 1754, there were over a thousand witch trials in Norway, and about 300 alleged witches and warlocks were executed or died in captivity, including 250 women and 50 men. The witches who were executed were burned at the stake or tied to a ladder that was pushed into a bonfire. The Lutheran theologians believed that the fire would cleanse the witches' souls and free them from the devil by burning away their sins. These gruesome executions were held in front of large crowds as a deterrent and a warning to others not to engage in witchcraft. Even young girls were tried and executed.

There was an unusually large number of witch trials and executions in Finnmark, the northernmost province of Norway. Despite its very small population, Finnmark was the site of 120 trials for witchcraft resulting in 91 deaths from execution or imprisonment. Most of the people executed in the western part of the province were

Sami male shamans, while female victims (both Norwegian and Sami) predominated in eastern Finnmark. In fact, it got to the point that so many women were arrested for witchcraft in Finnmark that they had their own dungeon called the witches' hole at the fortress in Vardø. Based on the flimsiest of charges and evidence, women were thrown into the witches' hole for weeks or months at a time in cold, deplorable conditions.

Government authorities and their accomplices in the Lutheran clergy used those inhumane conditions as well as torture and threats of torture to extract confessions from the accused women, all despite laws prohibiting torture before a death sentence. Instruments of torture included the rack and hot irons. Lutheran pastors were complicit in these activities, as they would occasionally stand next to the women and demand confessions while they were being tortured.

To determine if a confession was true, or to coerce a confession, the authorities sometimes subjected the accused women to the water ordeal. The woman's hands and feet were bound, and she was thrown into a lake or river or even the ocean. For the woman, it was a no-win proposition. If the accused floated on the surface of the water, it was concluded that she was a witch who should be executed. On the other hand, if she sank to the bottom, she would be found innocent, but then she would probably die from drowning.

Even after an accused woman confessed to witchcraft, she was often still subjected to inhumane treatment until she named other women who were also practicing witchcraft. Then the other women would be arrested and given the same treatment until they confessed and named more witches. These actions led to a series of chain trials in Finnmark, as more and more women were swept up by the authorities and accused, tried, and executed for witchcraft. As part of their confessions, the women were forced to tell how they had become witches and how they engaged in witchcraft. This led to some fantastic stories that were fabricated by the women in prison or at trial. There were many women in the witches' hole at any given time, and they would undoubtedly make up their stories together, which accounts for the similarity of their bizarre confessions.

For example, in 1620 a Sami woman called Finn-Kari was charged and arrested, and she confessed that she was a witch. She said that she was tempted by the devil who appeared to her in the form of a headless man, and that he handed her a beautiful bracelet that gave her the power to cast spells. Then he followed her around and tormented her if she did not practice witchcraft. She claimed to have caused several deaths, and in the water ordeal her confessions and guilt were confirmed when she floated like a cork. Just before being burned at the stake, she named two other witches, and that led the authorities to execute them and 10 other women that they accused in a series of trials. The same thing happened from time to time, as in 1651 when the confession of a woman named Gunnhild led to her own execution and the trials of 20 other women. In 1662 and 1663 about 30 women and girls were accused in witch trials in Finnmark. Chain trials of alleged witches were commonplace in Finnmark from 1620 to 1670.

In their confessions, accused women often spoke of regular gatherings (called sabbaths) of witches on remote mountaintops where they would worship the devil, drink a witch's brew or the devil's beer, and dance to the devil's music that he played on his red violin. They claimed they could ride through the sky on brooms or flying animals, or that they could transform themselves into birds, dogs, wolves, cats, goats, or sea monsters. They could create storms by blowing into a sack, tying it shut, and then releasing the knot to cause a strong wind. They caused shipwrecks by tying knots and rocks in clothing and then either throwing them at the ships before the voyage or chanting curses. In a 1662 trial, an accused witch named Sigrid described her relationship with a devil named Ole who had a black head with two horns and glowing eyes and who wore a pastor's robe. The accused women would usually confess to anything just to avoid further torment, even if it meant a certain death sentence.

The witch trials were a miscarriage of justice. Convictions were based on false or fabricated testimony and unlawful evidence. The accused hardly ever had a defense lawyer, and she had no opportunity to prepare a defense while sitting in the dungeon. The burden of proof was typically placed on the defendant, who had to produce multiple witnesses (who could not be members of her family) to testify that she was not a witch. This was virtually impossible, so there were few acquittals.

Although some of the Norwegian witchcraft laws remained in effect until 1842, the witch trials finally became less frequent in the late 1600s. At that point, more defendants were allowed to hire professional defense lawyers, and more knowledgeable and educated judges were appointed who refused to convict defendants based on superstition, the strange beliefs of religious authorities, false or unlawful testimony, or evidence obtained through torture or other cruel treatment. Norway's last execution for witchcraft occurred in 1695.

In 2011 the Queen of Norway unveiled the Steilneset Memorial in Vardø, dedicated to the 91 people who were killed for witchcraft in Finnmark, and concluding this terrible chapter in the history of Norway.

# CHAPTER TWELVE:
# *The Trumpet of Nordland*

*12. Fish drying racks in Lofoten*

PETTER DASS WAS A LUTHERAN PASTOR in Norway who wrote popular poems and hymns in the late 17th and early 18th centuries. He was born in Helgeland in the southern part of Nordland, was raised by his uncle (a pastor) after losing his parents, attended the Cathedral School in Trondheim, and studied theology at the University of Copenhagen. Returning to Helgeland, his budding career as a pastor faced a serious setback when he was found to have fathered an illegitimate child. Finally forgiven by the religious authorities, he became the parish pastor at Alstahaug, a position he held for many years.

Dass loved to travel around his beloved Nordland in Northern Norway, and he became known as the foremost Norwegian poet of his time. His masterwork was *Nordlands trompet* (*The Trumpet of Nordland*). It is an amazing epic poem that describes in great detail the landscape, homes, and people in all parts of Nordland, written in perfectly rhyming Danish (the written language of Norway at the time) with some Norwegian words and phrases. Dass worked on the poem from 1678 to 1700, and it was copied and read throughout Norway. He died before it was published in Norway and Denmark in the 1730s.

The following excerpt is an English version of part of the poem that describes the fishing communities in the Lofoten Islands. For centuries the Lofoten fishermen caught cod, hung them up to dry on wooden racks called *hjell* to preserve them, and then transported the dried fish (*stokkfisk*) all the way to Bergen for sale and export in exchange for money, grain, textiles, and other goods and supplies that they used in their daily lives. In some cases, the Bergen merchants provided the Lofoten fishermen with credit so they could obtain more goods purchased with fish to be delivered in the future. The last part of this excerpt describes a period of time when the Lofoten fishermen were struggling, and fish and credit were not readily available.


LAUNCH THE BOAT, turn the bow to the west, straight over the sea, for it will be best to sail with a favorable wind.

After we travel some 25 miles, I suddenly notice the fishing rich isle of Skrova is right there before us. There we cast anchor and wade into shore. We find drying racks and fishermen's huts all standing in rows.

The people are pleased with the plentiful cod in this place so renowned both here and abroad.

From Skrova to Vågan it's only six miles. So I sail there with haste on my fast-moving craft to find out what's there in the offing.

Arriving, I climb a small rise and like what I see. There are too many cabins for counting.

I look out to sea, see an incoming fleet, as much as three hundred in all. The fish they had caught they hang on the racks. As evening draws near, they finish their meals and head off to their sacks.

By early next morning, each tries to be first; they shove off their boats and are already gone, back to the sea.

The first one who reaches the fishing banks, he's always the champion and catches the most, while the last one gets only a few.

Each angler must bide his time and wait for the cod to start biting. You can't just tell the fish to come here, and they're not going to jump in the boat. So dangle your fish line many a time like your forefathers did before you.

I remember those years when Vågan and Skrova were famous each winter and spring; they would draw many common folk from round about. The men from all over Nordland would strive to go there with all their gear and their baggage.

From Helgeland, Salten, and Senjen they came, from Vesterål, Andenes, here and there, hoping to make a good living.

It was all their ambition to be in Vågan, to row and to fish. Vågan was always the talk of them all. When the fishing was best, the church made a haul by charging a tithe on their bounty,

But now the fish trade has never been worse; it seems to have all gone way in reverse, and the ocean is keeping its riches.

Here nothing has prospered for ten years or so, for poverty strikes them all high and all low, so no one can make a good living.

The cabins are rotting, the racks falling down; you don't see the cargo ships, sails or masts; it's like the place is deserted.

When the fish disappear, the Lofoten man must sit anxiously by in his sauna. Like a bird in flight, he has nothing to plant or to harvest or save for the future.

All that he owns is a well-worn boat, some bait, and a hook, an old leather coat, a sweater, and patched-up britches. That's all he has to fill wants and needs, with that he must live and pay taxes.

His plow and his field, his forge and his yoke, they all hang together on one single hook when all the fish are biting.

But when fishing has failed him again, then he and his woman and their hired hand, they go hungry to bed from the table, for their miserable lives they must suffer.

He travels to Bergen to get a new loan, but creditors sense he has little to give, so they could not make any money.

With each passing year he goes more in arrears, so it goes when the Lord wants to punish.

# CHAPTER THIRTEEN:
# *Farmers and their Fields*

13. A farm family in Gol in 1699

BY THE 1700S Norway had finally recovered from the Black Death. The country's population in 1700 was back to about the same level as in 1300 before the plague. The population continued to grow from about 500,000 to 900,000 in the 18th century. Although there were fishermen along the coast and merchants and tradesmen in the towns and small cities, the vast majority of Norwegians were farmers, and Norway was a relatively poor agricultural society. The farms that had been deserted in the

Black Death were now reoccupied, and less desirable land was being cleared for new farms.

At that time, there were four classes of farmers in Norway. First, a minority of farmers called *selveiere* (singular: *selveier*) owned their own farms under a registered deed. Sometimes they leased part of their land to other farmers. There were wealthy selveiere who owned extensive lands, but most selveiere had modest or small farms. Some of the farms had been purchased from the crown in the 1600s when the kings of Denmark and Norway were desperate for funds to finance their frequent wars against Sweden and other countries. Under Norway's inheritance laws, alodial rights attached to most of these farms. That is, when the owner of a farm died, his oldest son inherited the farm, but he had to provide some compensation to his siblings. If he tried to sell the farm to someone who was not a member of the family, his family could redeem and reacquire the farm.

Second, there were also farmers called *leilendinger* (singular: *leilending*) who each leased an entire farm from the owner under a registered lease. The owners who leased the farms to leilendinger were other farmers, or the crown, or merchants or wealthy landowners in local towns or cities who had purchased the lands from the crown. The leilendinger did not have alodial rights or obligations, but their descendants normally inherited their leasehold interests in the farms.

The leilendinger had pretty much the same social status as the selveiere, but both classes of farmers had to bear a heavy burden of expenses. Apart from the costs of running the farm and supporting his family, a selveier or leilending was obligated to pay substantial taxes to the government and tithes to the church. Of course, the leilending also had to pay rent to the owner. So even though the selveiere and the leilendinger made up the highest class of Norwegian farmers, they were not generally considered to be part of the upper class of Norwegian society.

On the farm, the men were responsible for working the fields and raising the livestock, and they hunted and fished for additional food. Some farmers also worked as blacksmiths, carpenters, or craftsmen, making and repairing household items and farm implements for others in order to earn more money. The women did all the work inside the farmhouse, such as cleaning, raising the children, making and washing clothes, preparing meals, and churning butter. The women were also expected to feed and milk the cows or goats and help with the harvesting of crops. On most farms, it was a life of hard work for both men and women. Their homes were generally well-maintained, and they gradually began to enjoy improved living conditions with ovens, fireplaces, and chimneys (instead of the old open hearths with holes in the ceiling to let the smoke escape), as well as wooden floors, glass windows, and better furniture.

The *husmenn* (singular: *husmann*) made up the third class of farmers. Although the practices varied in different parts of Norway, a typical husmann had a lifetime lease of a small plot of land on a farm. Unlike a leilending, a husmann did not lease an entire farm. The husmann's plot was often located in a remote, less desirable part of the farm. There were usually a few buildings on the husmann's small plot, such as a ramshackle cabin and a small barn. Some husmenn only leased a cabin and not any land. The husmann paid rent to the owner or leilending, either in the form of money or more often by providing farm labor. The husmann did not have to pay real estate taxes because his small plot was not listed on the tax rolls. Instead, it was the owner or leilending who paid the real estate tax on the entire farm that included the husmann's plot. The husmann usually owned just a few cows or goats for milk, and when not working for the landlord he raised a few crops on his plot of land. In addition, husmenn often had to work other jobs as lumbermen, fishermen, miners, or tradesmen, just to make ends meet. A husmann was poor and a member of the lower class of society with little or no opportunity to ever improve his prospects in life. His wife could stay on the plot after he died, but his children normally had no right to inherit the husmann's place.

Some husmenn had written leases with the owners or leilendinger, but in many cases there was nothing more than an oral agreement and a handshake. In the absence of written agreements, some husmenn were kicked off their plots if the owner or leilending wanted the land back, or if the owner or leilending claimed that the husmann had not complied with the oral lease. Some husmenn were unlawfully terminated and evicted even if they acted in accordance with a written lease. From time to time the king issued new laws to protect the rights of the husmenn.

A good example of a husmann's lease is the following contract between an owner and a husmann in Gudbrandsdalen in 1795:

> I, Marthe Skarstad, have assigned to Jens Knudsen and his wife Lisbeth Halvorsdatter a piece of land at Skarstadhagen, 6/10 of an acre, to clear and build a place at my farm Skarstad for their lifetimes. They will pay me (or whoever owns the farm) an annual fee by plowing 1-1/2 acres in the field, by mowing grain for 2 weeks, and by harvest work for 1 week in the fall. If I ask him, he will also work for me for daily compensation: 8 shillings per day with the scythe; or 8 shillings for plowing; 8 shillings to cut down trees; or 6 shillings for work at midsummer; and 4 shillings per day between the end of harvest and the 14th of April. He may use a piece of pasture land on the meadow called Odden, and his animals may graze there as long as the animals from the main farm graze there in the spring and fall. He may enjoy and farm the above-described place and make use of it as he best knows.

Under this lease, the husmann and his wife obtained the right to live on a small plot of raw land during their lifetimes. It was up to them to clear the land and build a cabin and other buildings there. They paid rent to the owner by working on her farm for a certain length of time each year. She could require them to work more, but then she had to pay them specified amounts of compensation for the additional work. This compensation received by the husmann was usually less than the owner paid to her own farm hands for the same work. The husmann could use his plot as he saw fit, such as by raising some crops and livestock, and his livestock could graze on part of the owner's land.

So the husmann had a place to live and a means to eke out a basic existence. The owner received cheap labor by allowing the husmann to live on a small piece of land that the owner was probably not using anyway. As farmland became scarce or unavailable in much of Norway, and as the population grew, thousands of farmers had to become husmenn, and by 1800 one-third of all the farmers in Norway were husmenn.

Although they were poor, the husmenn did not make up the lowest class of the agricultural society in Norway. That was reserved for the fourth and least fortunate class of farmers – the farm hands, each called an *innerst*. The innerst was a common farm laborer who did not own or lease any land. He was paid by the owner or leilending of the farm for his labor, and he could be fired at any time. If he was lucky, he was allowed to eat and sleep in the farmhouse. More often, the farm hands would eat and sleep in shared small huts on the farm or in the barn. Sometimes farm hands and servant girls both slept in the same barn, with the girls on the ground floor and the farm hands in the loft. They got to know each other, and that contributed to the increase in population. Many farm hands lived in abject poverty and owned nothing more than the clothes on their backs and their old cooking pots. Some of them roamed the countryside looking for work.

Norway continued to have four classes of farmers well into the 1800s, when many of them migrated to the cities for work or left Norway for a new life in America.

# CHAPTER FOURTEEN:
# *Merchants and Privateers*

*14. A jekt cargo ship from Nordland*

The city of Trondheim, formerly called Nidaros, grew from a small village in Viking times to the residence of King Olav Tryggvason in the late 10th century to the seat of the archbishop and the Church of Norway beginning in 1152. Still, for many years thereafter, Trondheim was a sleepy little town dominated by the great Nidaros Cathedral but overshadowed by the larger city of

Bergen, which became the center of government and trade in Norway as early as the 12th century. For hundreds of years, Bergen had a monopoly on trade with Northern Norway, and foreign ships were not permitted to sail north of Bergen.

However, that monopoly ended in 1715 with the result that Trondheim became a prosperous trading center in the 18th century. Merchants moved to Trondheim from Bergen and other countries, and Norwegian and foreign ships filled Trondheim's harbor, bringing textiles, grain, and other goods from abroad in exchange for fish from Northern Norway, timber from Trøndelag and other inland areas, and copper from Røros.

Over time there arose an upper class of merchants and public officials in Trondheim. They established trading firms, built and owned ships, and constructed factories in the city for sugar and liquor refining, tobacco folding, ironworking, and other industries. A partnership of wealthy Trondheim merchants owned the profitable Røros Copper Works. At home the merchants spoke Danish or German and lived in mansions. Their wives and daughters wore the latest European fashions. The upper class also imported literature, newspapers, and cultural and political ideas from Europe.

The most prominent member of the upper crust in Trondheim was Hans Carl Knudtzon. Originally from Slesvig in Southern Denmark, he arrived in Trondheim in 1767 and founded what became a very successful trading house. He owned over 20 ships, and he was part owner of the sugar refinery, the Røros partnership, and other businesses. He and his family frequently traveled abroad. His daughter was married in France, and his sons studied in Germany. Knudtzon's ships sailed all over the world, sometimes on voyages that lasted for several years.

Trondheim merchants prospered during the first 15 years of the Napoleonic Wars from 1792 to 1807. The Kingdom of Denmark and Norway was neutral and could trade with countries on both sides of the conflict. Norwegians could charge high prices for their exports and high freight rates for goods carried on their ships.

Unfortunately, that period of prosperity ended abruptly in 1807 when Britain attacked Denmark, the King of Denmark and Norway joined Napoleon's alliance against the British, and Britain sent its navy ships and privateers to blockade the ports of Norway. The privateers were privately-owned pirate ships that were licensed and authorized by the British government to participate in the blockade and attack and capture Norwegian ships. The blockade covered the entire coastline of Norway from the south to the far north, and it continued for much of the next seven years until 1814. The British even attacked towns in Northern Norway such as Hammerfest.

The blockade was a serious problem for the merchants of Trondheim. They could not import or export any goods, and their ships were being attacked and commandeered at sea. It was even more serious for the people of Northern Norway. They could no longer ship their dried fish to Trondheim, Bergen, or Denmark, and they could not import grain to feed their families. For centuries the northern fishermen had sent their cargo ships called *jekter* (singular: *jekt*) filled with fish to ports farther south where they would trade the fish for grain and other products. The blockade made this very difficult, and the people of Northern Norway began to starve. Without flour, they had to make bread from ground-up pine bark, Iceland moss, or lichen. Some Norwegian vessels made it through the blockade at night or by outrunning the British ships, but most did not, and many Norwegian ships, cargoes, and sailors were captured by the British. Some Norwegian sailors had to spend years in captivity on prison ships in British ports.

The merchants of Trondheim and the fishermen of Northern Norway made efforts to counteract the blockade. Denmark-Norway entered into a treaty with Russia that allowed Norwegians to import grain from Archangel in Northern Russia, but that worked only if ships could avoid the blockade. Furthermore, trade with Russia ended when Napoleon invaded Russia in 1812 and Russia joined the British alliance. Trondheim merchants like Knudtzon converted some of their ships to privateers after receiving licenses signed by the King of

Denmark and Norway that authorized them to attack and seize British ships on the high seas. The blockade turned into an ongoing battle between the British navy and British privateers on one side and Norwegian privateers and a few Norwegian navy gunboats on the other side.

On the Norwegian side, there were some success stories and tales of heroism. On one occasion an unarmed Norwegian jekt from Northern Norway had delivered dried fish to Bergen and was loaded with goods on its voyage back home to Vesterålen when it was approached by a small but fully armed British boat. The cargo of the jekt included two large millstones. The British vessel ordered the jekt to lower its sails. But when the British came alongside the jekt and were ready to board and capture the Norwegians and their vessel and cargo, the crew of the jekt suddenly lifted the heavy millstones and hoisted them into the British boat. The millstones crashed through the hull of the British vessel, creating two large holes in the bottom of the boat. The Brits who tried to board the jekt were beaten back with handspikes and other implements, and they ended up in the sea. The British boat promptly sank, and the Norwegians escaped and sailed safely to Vesterålen with all of their cargo except for the two millstones.

Farther south, the British navy had captured or sunk almost the entire Danish fleet in their invasion of Denmark in 1807. The Norwegian navy had nothing more than some small gunboats that were built at several places along the Norwegian coast with money and other valuables collected from the local population. The crews of the gunboats tried to protect Norwegian cargo ships from the much larger ships of the British navy and British privateers. At the Battle of Alvøen in May 1808, a large British navy frigate unlawfully flying a Dutch flag tried to sneak into the harbor at Bergen and was surprised by five Norwegian gunboats. The Norwegians opened fire, damaged the frigate, and killed 12 Brits including the captain of the frigate. The frigate surrendered, but then fled with a favorable wind before it could be boarded. Nevertheless, the battle was a rare victory for the

Norwegians, and thereafter it deterred the British from operating too close to the Norwegian coastline.

The blockade was finally lifted in 1814 when Sweden, Denmark, and Britain signed the Treaty of Kiel, which transferred Norway from the King of Denmark to the King of Sweden. In response, the Norwegians drafted their own constitution and declared their independence on the 17th of May 1814 (*syttende mai*). However, later that same year Norway was forced to join a union with Sweden, although Norway got to keep its own constitution and control over its domestic affairs. That union lasted until 1905, when Norway became a fully independent country.

Knudtzon was initially opposed to the union with Sweden, but he became a member of the first Norwegian legislature called the *Storting* that approved the union. He was also part of the Norwegian delegation that traveled to Stockholm to inform the Swedish king that he had been elected King of Norway and to give the king a copy of Norway's amended constitution that recognized the union. In 1815 Knudtzon and his wife hosted a lavish dinner party for Karl Johan, the Swedish Crown Prince who subsequently was crowned in Stockholm and Trondheim as the King of Sweden and Norway.

# CHAPTER FIFTEEN:

## *Oleana*

*15. A Norwegian pioneer schoolhouse in Wisconsin*

NORWAY EXPERIENCED A MASS EXODUS of its people in the 1800s and early 1900s. Between 1825 and 1929, as many as a million Norwegians left their native land to make a hazardous journey across the sea to an uncertain future in America. Each Norwegian had one or more reasons to seek a new life in the New World. Some of the most common reasons were the following.

First, until the 1840s there was no religious freedom in Norway except for members of the Lutheran state church. So some of the early emigrants, including Haugians and Quakers, moved to the United States where they could freely practice their religions and avoid religious and social persecution.

Second, until the 1870s the Norwegian government, including the king's Cabinet, the Storting and the national and local bureaucracy, was dominated by an upper class of public officials. The farmers considered those officials to be arrogant foreigners who spoke Danish, raised the farmers' taxes, and paid themselves handsomely while the farmers struggled to make ends meet. The farmers also resented the fact that all the public officials had voting rights while only a fraction of the farmers were allowed to vote, the officials were exempt from military service but the farmers had to serve in the army or navy, and in bad economic times it was the officials who foreclosed on the farms. This resentment was so great that many farmers left Norway to live in a country where hopefully they would not feel like servants of the government officials.

Third, and most importantly, Norway's population doubled from about 900,000 to 1,800,000 during the period from 1810 to 1875. This spectacular growth was the result of a substantial drop in the death rate. Beginning in 1810, everyone was required to receive the smallpox vaccine, so there were fewer epidemics. At the same time, educated midwives were hired by the local communities throughout Norway, as required by law, and they assisted mothers and their babies in childbirth. There was better nutrition as the potato and herring became standard components of the diet. Most Norwegians enjoyed better living conditions. Later in the century, there was better sanitation, including cleaner streets, once the medical profession figured out that most disease was caused by bacteria. All of these factors resulted in longer lives for all Norwegians.

Due to the substantial increase in population, there was no vacant farmland left in Southern and Central Norway, and there were not enough jobs to go around. Norway had a stratified class society where the members of the lower class had no opportunity to improve themselves. As their numbers grew, theirs was a life of poverty and hopelessness in Norway. If a poor husmann, farm hand, or servant could somehow scrape together enough money, he or she could book passage on a ship across the Atlantic to what had to be a better life in America. A poor farmer or servant in Norway could purchase a farm on the fertile Midwestern prairie for next to nothing and finally have a chance to lead a decent life.

Fourth, there were tough economic times, famines, floods, and generally bad weather in Norway throughout much of the 19th century, whereas the American economy was normally much healthier. While the Industrial Revolution in the late 1800s provided some new jobs in the cities and towns of Norway, the wages for industrial workers were higher in the United States. After 1865, tens of thousands of Norwegians emigrated in years when Norway's economy was struggling and there were favorable economic times in America.

Fifth, as the 1800s progressed, there was better transportation in Norway, across the ocean, and in the U.S. There were new macadam roads, railroads, and coastal steamers in Norway, which made it easier for emigrants to leave their remote homes and travel to the port cities. By the 1860s, more comfortable steamships were replacing the old sailing ships, and the duration of the ocean voyage was reduced from one or two months to just two weeks. The steamship tickets became cheaper because of more competition between steamship lines. Also by the 1860s, railroads were being built all over the U.S. So a Norwegian emigrant could leave home in Norway and reach his or her final destination in the New World much faster than ever before.

Sixth, many Norwegians went to America for personal reasons. These included lost love affairs, arguments with family members or neighbors, disputes with landlords, pregnancy, or divorce. Some people left to avoid paying their creditors or to escape criminal prosecution. A few Norwegian communities heartlessly paid to send poverty-stricken people across the ocean so they would not be a burden on the welfare system in Norway.

Seventh, Norwegians were constantly receiving letters from friends and loved ones in America, encouraging them to come to the New World. Some letters included prepaid steamship tickets or promises of land, housing, or employment. In a small community in Norway, it was quite an event if someone received a letter from America. Frequently all the neighbors would get together to read the letter and find out the latest news about family and friends in the U.S. Many letters were published in newspapers or magazines. While not all the letters were positive, most of them painted a bright picture of America as the land of opportunity. It was much easier for someone to leave Norway if he or she expected to be welcomed by familiar faces at the ultimate destination.

Eighth, some people left Norway simply because it was the thing to do. They caught what was called America fever or emigration fever. That is, if a Norwegian watched most of his family, friends, and acquaintances leave for America, he or she was more inclined to follow them, whether or not there was a good reason to do so.

Finally, there were steamship companies, railroad companies, mining companies, and land speculators who had agents all over Norway to encourage people to move to America. The steamship companies wanted to sell tickets. The American railroads and land speculators were offering land at cheap prices. The American mining companies were looking for new employees. Their agents advertised in the press, and distributed brochures and handbills in their offices and on the streets. Norwegians were literally flooded with information telling them how wonderful it would be to go to America.

Of course, not all of the promises of those companies, speculators, and agents turned out to be true, much to the dismay of Norwegians who made the long journey only to be left in the lurch in an unfamiliar country. One such land speculator whose promises did not come true was the renowned Norwegian musician Ole Bull.

Ole Bull was a violin virtuoso, a world-famous musician and composer from Norway who went on several successful concert tours throughout Europe and America. He was also a Norwegian patriot who loved his native land, and he based much of his repertoire and many of his compositions on Norwegian folk melodies, which he also shared with his young protégé Edvard Grieg.

But in addition, Ole Bull was a person who had strong democratic ideals. He experienced the 1848 revolution in Paris, and he hoped that it would change the social and political conditions in Norway, where members of the lower class were third-class citizens who were poor, had no right to vote, and could not improve their lives.

When there was no change in Norway, he was very disappointed, and he came up with a solution. He formulated a plan to create an egalitarian colony of Norwegians in the New World, or as he put it, "a New Norway dedicated to freedom, baptized in independence, and protected by the mighty flag of the Union." He was, of course, referring to the United States.

So in 1851, on a concert tour in America, Ole Bull looked at some properties for his new colony in the Eastern United States, before purchasing 11,144 acres in a remote corner of northern Pennsylvania, sight unseen, from a land speculator and a lawyer in New York City. The property featured a beautiful landscape, a valley in rugged mountains that reminded him of Norway. He started building his own mansion called *Slottet* (the palace), and he made grand plans for a cannon factory, sawmills, a hotel, and even a polytechnic school, with jobs for thousands of Norwegians. The cannon factory would produce guns to be sold to the U.S. Army in California. There would be a church, a school, and other amenities, and lots for hundreds of homesteads. He also negotiated with two railroad companies to extend their lines to the settlement, and he had ideas to build more towns with names such as New Bergen and Walhalla.

Then he started advertising in Norway to draw settlers to his New Norway. He promised each of them $15 per month salary (or $30 for skilled tradesmen), plus free food and lodging, and cheap land for farming. A few Norwegian newspaper editors took up the cause and enthusiastically encouraged Norwegians to go there. The socialist editor Marcus Thrane described Ole Bull as a man of freedom who wanted to improve the lot of poor Norwegians, and he published the following song: "He knows that here is grief and need. He wants to lift your burdens. He'll give you freedom and bread; he wants to ease your living. You know the man – it's Ole Bull!"

On September 5, 1852, Ole Bull raised the colony's new flag – a combination of the Norwegian, Swedish, and American flags – on a tall evergreen tree at the settlement, and he christened the colony Oleana, named after himself. Two days later the first 30 Norwegians arrived, and a couple hundred more followed them there over the next few months. During the first month, there were nightly celebrations at Oleana, with singing, violin music by the maestro, speeches, and food, but no alcohol except for wine because Ole Bull wanted an alcohol-free settlement. He even bought 150 silk top hats for the male settlers to wear at holiday celebrations.

Unfortunately, within a month, things started to go haywire in paradise. Ole Bull was running short on funds. He wanted to reduce the settlers' wages, but they angrily refused. So he arranged an impromptu concert tour to raise more money.

One of the problems was that the settlement was in a very remote place in the middle of nowhere, and it was very difficult to get there. The railroad lines were never built. Ole Bull made the same mistake as many other early Norwegian settlers in America by choosing to live in a beautiful place that looked like Norway but was totally unsuitable for farming, industry, or just about anything else. The narrow valley at Oleana was surrounded by steep mountains covered with forests that were nearly impossible to clear. There was hardly any level land for farming. The red, sandy soil was not fertile. The local Norwegian pastor came up with an apt description, stating that the place was only fit to be a goat farm. Furthermore, Ole Bull was charging the settlers twice as much for land as the going rate farther west. A sawmill was built, but without any transportation there was no way to take the lumber to market.

Ole Bull returned to Oleana in May 1853, only to find that some settlers had already left for more promising land in Wisconsin and Minnesota, and the rest of the settlers were about ready to follow them. Ole Bull tried to raise their spirits by holding lavish celebrations on the 17th of May and the 4th of July. But that was the end of his dream because that summer almost all of the settlers departed. Ole Bull did not even complete the construction of his own house. By September 1853 he left Oleana, sold the land back to the original owners, and incurred a substantial loss of as much as $70,000. Oleana went bust, and only two Norwegians stuck it out and remained at the settlement.

Various Norwegian newspaper editors had always been skeptical of Ole Bull's project, and now they jumped at the chance to heap scorn on him and his failed settlement. In many articles, they made fun of his exaggerated promises of a New Norway that never materialized.

Ditmar Meidell, the editor of a satirical Norwegian magazine in Christiania (Oslo) called *Krydseren*, wrote several critical columns about Bull and Oleana, including one in which he proposed sarcastically that all of Norway should be moved to America where the Norwegians could establish several new states – not just Oleana, but also Mariana, Larsiana, and Påliana. For a time, Ole Bull and his failed settlement became the laughingstock of Norway. Even his friend Henrik Ibsen, in his play *Peer Gynt*, mentioned a settlement called Gyntiana that his lead character foolishly wanted to establish.

Meidell's articles also featured a parody song about Oleana that became popular for many years in Norway and the U.S., and it was sung more recently by the American folk singer Pete Seeger. Here is an English translation of some of Meidell's verses in the song.

It's good to be in Oleana instead of bearing the chains of slavery in
    Norway.
In Oleana the land is free, and the grain grows fast there, too.
The crops haul themselves into the barn while I lie down in my
    bedroom and rest.

The beer's as good as one can brew, and it flows down the streams for every poor man to enjoy.

The salmon are jumping in the creek; when you call them they hop right into your cooking pot for you to serve.

Roasted pigs run about, and politely ask if anyone would like some ham to eat.

The calves skin and butcher and fry themselves quicker than you can take a swig.

The hens lay eggs as big as a house while the rooster keeps time like an eight days' clock.

You earn two dollars a day to pay for your booze, and if you're really lazy you might get four.

The wife and kids are supported by the town, and if they don't pay they get punched in the nose.

We go around in velvet clothes with silver buttons, and the wife fills my fancy pipe so I can smoke it.

Yes, if you really want to live, go to Oleana; the poorest wretch in Norway is a duke over there.

# CHAPTER SIXTEEN:
# *The Great Lockout*

## Forhandlernes forslag til hovedavtale med Norsk Arbeidsgiverforening.

*16. Union announcement of proposed labor agreement in 1935*

FTER THE FIRST WORLD WAR ENDED IN 1918, Norway no longer enjoyed a preferred economic position as a neutral country that could trade with and ship goods for all countries, including those on both sides of the war. There was a worldwide postwar depression, and a serious economic downturn in Norway that continued from time to time throughout the 1920s and early 1930s. There were low prices and less demand for Norwegian products. Many businesses failed, and rampant unemployment and hardship gripped the country.

The socialist workers' unions in Norway reacted to the economic crisis by becoming more radical. They pledged to foment a workers' revolution followed by a dictatorship of the proletariat, like what their comrades the Bolsheviks had accomplished in Russia. The rest of the Norwegian population and their political leaders who controlled the Norwegian government were fearful of a workers' revolution, and therefore they took actions to suppress worker demonstrations and strikes.

In a typical scenario that occurred periodically, during an economic downturn the employers tried to reduce the workers' wages, the unions refused and went on strike, the employers instituted a lockout of union workers and hired nonunion workers, and there were confrontations between the union workers and the police that tried to protect the strikebreakers. On occasion the government sent the military to assist the police and prevent violence. When the dust settled, the employers and the unions negotiated a pay cut, and the union workers went back to their jobs with less money than before.

Reduced wages and periods of unemployment led to widespread poverty among the working class. Their families did not have enough food to eat, and their children sometimes had to attend school in ragged clothing without shoes. Some local communities started public works projects to put the unemployed back to work, and the welfare system was expanded to provide public assistance and food stamps to the poor.

Then things got worse. In October 1929 the American stock market crashed, and the Great Depression spread from the U.S. to the rest of the world. The depression hit Norway in the fall of 1930, and once again there were failed businesses, labor strife, and unemployment. By December 1932, 42 percent of the union workforce in Norway was unemployed. The economic problems caused some cities such as Kristiansund to go bust. And the vicious cycle of wage reductions, strikes, lockouts, strikebreakers, and confrontations continued, culminating in the Menstad conflict in 1931.

Early that year, the Norwegian national organization of employers responded to the economic crisis by announcing a general pay cut of 15 to 20 percent. The workers' national trade union rejected the pay cut and instead proposed a temporary reduction of working hours. The parties were at an impasse, and there were massive strikes in some industries. In February the employers announced a nationwide lockout of union workers. Tens of thousands of Norwegians were suddenly out of work.

Norsk Hydro, one of the largest companies in Norway, had a plant and shipping facility at Menstad near Skien in Telemark. As a major employer, Norsk Hydro joined the nationwide lockout, and in April 1931 the company hired nonunion contract workers to fill the jobs of the laid-off union workers. It was not difficult for Norsk Hydro to find nonunion workers to sign a three-month labor contract because there were so many unemployed people who were desperate for a job and money to support their families. The union leaders at Norsk Hydro asked the contract workers to stop working, but they refused because they did not want to lose their jobs. The situation became extremely tense as the union workers called the contract workers scabs and traitors to the working class.

The Communists had broken away from the socialist Labor Party and formed their own Communist Party in 1923. Although the Communists had lost all of their seats in the Storting and almost all of their nationwide political support by 1931, they still wielded influence and held leadership positions in the unions.

At Menstad the Communists began to organize mass demonstrations by the union workers. On May 22 about 1,500 workers marched through the streets of Skien carrying signs that condemned the lockout and the strikebreakers. Labor Party leaders appeared at Skien and Porsgrunn and gave inspired speeches, but the Communists were not satisfied with mere words. They wanted to incite the workers into more aggressive actions. On May 30 the Communists led a union march to the docks, intending to stop the work of the strikebreakers. They succeeded, and Norsk Hydro sent the contract workers home for the day. That confrontation led to some harsh words and physical jostling between the union and nonunion workers.

This situation was unacceptable to the management of Norsk Hydro, which asked the police to start protecting the contract workers and their right to work under lawful contracts. That put the local police in a difficult position. They wanted to keep the peace without alienating either side.

On June 2 the Communists led another march, this time with 1,200 union workers waving red flags. After breaking through two gates at the Norsk Hydro plant, the workers stopped temporarily in front of a line of police. But shortly thereafter they broke through a fence and stormed the Norsk Hydro office building where some contract workers were hiding. The union workers dragged out the contract workers and swore and spit at them before the police were able to come to their rescue and walk them to their homes.

In Oslo, the Norwegian government was led by ultra-conservatives such as Defense Minister Vidkun Quisling, the future leader of the Norwegian Nazi party. The government strongly supported Norsk Hydro and condemned the union demonstrators at Menstad. At a June 3 meeting of the Justice Minister and representatives of the employers' organization and Norsk Hydro, it was decided that 150 state policemen would be sent to Porsgrunn to control the situation at Menstad. The Justice Minister also ordered the local police chief in Skien to stop the demonstrations and to enable the contract workers to continue their jobs. The Skien police chief objected to this harder line against the union workers, so the Justice Minister replaced him with a police officer named Annar Thinn from Moss, who had prior experience in dealing with workers' demonstrations.

When Thinn and the state police arrived at Porsgrunn, the Communist-led workers blockaded and threw rocks at the hotel where they were staying. In the meantime, the Communists planned a much stronger action in a final confrontation with the police and the strikebreakers. They prepared for a march to Menstad, armed the workers with iron bars, chains, poles, and rocks, and placed the largest, strongest workers on the front line.

On June 8 about 2,000 workers marched to Menstad, where 10 contract workers were protected by a line of 100 policemen and police cadets led by Thinn. The police officer from Moss had armed his men with nightsticks. He was determined to teach the union workers a lesson and end the demonstrations once and for all. As they approached the Norsk Hydro facility, the demonstrators were waving red flags, and two union bands were playing *The Internationale*, the socialist anthem. When they got a few yards from the police line, the workers stopped when ordered to do so by Thinn. But some demonstrators then started to push forward, and others began to throw rocks at the police. At that point, Thinn ordered the police to spray the demonstrators with fire hoses, and in the confusion he then ordered the police to charge the demonstrators. Pandemonium broke loose as an all-out brawl erupted between the police and the demonstrators, accompanied by music played by the bands. The two sides hit each other with their weapons, and more rocks were thrown, including some by union wives who were standing nearby. Soon the outnumbered police were overwhelmed. Three policemen were seriously injured, one lost an eye, and the rest of them fled the scene.

The melee only lasted five minutes. The police regrouped and rearmed themselves, but the demonstrators did not pursue them. Instead they turned around and marched in a victory parade to the athletic field where they held a rally.

When the government found out what happened at Menstad, they immediately sent 390 armed soldiers and sailors and four warships to Skien. The police units were strengthened and armed with teargas guns. The military arrived on June 9, and their presence defused the situation. There were no more demonstrations at Menstad. On June 14 the police began to arrest the leaders of the June 8 demonstration, and 20 of them were later sentenced to jail terms of 30 days to 10 months. The Communists called for a general strike of all the workers in the area, but they were voted down. Norsk Hydro gave the contract workers an eight-week vacation and then terminated the contract worker program. The nationwide general lockout ended in September 1931, and the union workers returned to their jobs.

The Menstad conflict was the last serious confrontation between employers and workers in Norway. The economic depression continued for four more years, and there were still occasional workers' strikes. But they were settled through negotiation and compromise. By 1935 the Norwegian economy gradually began to improve. In that same year, employers and workers entered into a landmark, comprehensive labor agreement, and a more moderate Labor Party formed its first national government in Norway. The Labor government enacted legislation that broadened workers' benefits under the welfare system while also providing financial assistance to a recovering Norwegian economy.

# CHAPTER SEVENTEEN:
# *The Old Fisherman Who Defied the Nazis*

*17. Beautiful Ålesund*

NAZI GERMANY INVADED NORWAY at several places along the coast on April 9, 1940, and occupied the entire country within two months. The occupation continued for five years until the Germans surrendered in 1945 to end the Second World War in Europe. Norwegians reacted in different ways to the occupation. Just about everyone was shocked that Norway, a neutral country, was taken over by a foreign power just 35 years after the Norwegians had finally achieved their independence in 1905. Some fought against the Germans or joined underground organizations, including those who were subsequently captured by the Nazis, tortured, and imprisoned or executed. Hundreds of Norwegian Jews escaped to Sweden, while many others were killed in concentration camps. The king, crown prince, and government of Norway fled the country and set up a government-in-exile in London. Other Norwegians collaborated with the Germans, and tens of thousands joined the Norwegian Nazi party led by Vidkun Quisling. Most people in Norway tried to continue their daily lives and cope with the occupation, the police state, and the rationing that lasted until Germany was defeated by the Allies and Norwegian democracy was restored.

This is the extraordinary story of an ordinary Norwegian, an elderly fisherman, who just did what he felt he had to do, and opposed the Nazis in the first few weeks after the German invasion of Norway.

IN THE SPRING OF 1940, Ole Solbjørg was an 80-year old fishing boat captain in Ålesund on the west coast of Norway. Ole owned three boats. When the Germans occupied Ålesund in early May, he decided that he wanted no part of them. So he made plans to leave the country. On May 3 he gathered a crew of volunteers, and they sailed his boat called the *Utvær* out of the harbor and on to the British-controlled Faeroe Islands, where they arrived two days later.

Ole figured that the war would not last very long, but for the time being he wanted to continue fishing. However, he could not find any fishing equipment for sale in the Faeroes, so he thought it best to sail back to Norway, pick up some equipment, and see if it was possible to bring his other two boats to the Faeroes. He decided to leave the *Utvær* in the Faeroes and take a small open dory with a sail and motor across the sea to Norway, and he needed another man to go with him.

Everyone in the Faeroes thought that Ole was crazy to sail back to German-occupied Norway in a small boat, and it was difficult for him to find someone to join him. But he finally located a man who wanted to go to Norway and fetch his family. Someone warned Ole that the man liked to drink and that liquor made him very unpleasant, but Ole didn't think too much of it. He did, however, hide the man's liquor under a floorboard of the boat before they left.

Unfortunately, the weather did not cooperate on the voyage back to Norway. As they approached the Norwegian coast, they ran into a bad storm that pushed them back out to sea, and then the motor conked out. As if that were not enough, the other man got hold of his liquor, became extremely hostile, and at one point tried to throw Ole overboard. It was only Ole's expert seamanship that brought them through the storm and saved their lives. As they neared the coast of Norway once again, they were met by an old acquaintance of Ole's in a boat, and he directed them through a German minefield to the island of Maløy quite a ways south of Ålesund. There they repaired the motor, and then they sailed to Ålesund, where an exhausted Ole went to sleep in his bed for days.

When he awoke, Ole was informed that his boat called the *Eidøy* was in Flekkefjord way down in Southern Norway. He gathered a small crew, avoided the Germans, and sailed the dory to Flekkefjord. They boarded the *Eidøy*, sailed it back to Ålesund, and loaded it with fishing equipment and supplies. Then the crew, following Ole's instructions, sailed the *Eidøy* out of Ålesund harbor in the fog right under the noses of the Germans. They took the boat to the Faeroes.

Ole stayed in Ålesund, where his third boat called the *Gå På* was located. He loaded that boat with more equipment and provisions. But by then the residents of Ålesund had begun to talk about Ole and his exploits. The Germans got wind of it, and they decided to keep watch over Ole's boat and arrest him if he showed up. So Ole went into hiding.

One night the Germans stayed on board the *Gå På* until 11 o'clock. At that point they decided that Ole would not be returning to the boat in the middle of the night, so they left. From a hiding place, Ole watched the Germans leave the boat. Shortly after the Germans were out of sight, Ole and his crew boarded the *Gå På* and calmly sailed the boat out of the harbor to the Faeroe Islands.

So Ole and his crews managed to escape from the Nazis multiple times with all three of his boats, and Ole continued fishing for the rest of the war. Word of Ole's daring deeds spread along the west coast of Norway, and he was an inspiration to members of the Norwegian resistance who also avoided the Germans and sailed boats between Norway and the British-occupied Faeroe and Shetland Islands throughout the war.

When the war ended in 1945, at the age of 85, Ole returned on the *Gå På* to celebrations in Ålesund. For his brave efforts, Ole received the St. Olav's Medal.

# CHAPTER EIGHTEEN:
# *Carl Fredriksens Transport*

*18. Last stretch of the road to Sweden used by Carl Fredriksens Transport*

A FTER NAZI GERMANY INVADED and occupied Norway in the spring of 1940, many Norwegian Jews fled the country to freedom in Sweden. During World War II Sweden was a neutral country and therefore a safe haven for refugees from Norway. But when the Nazis did not persecute the remaining Jews in Norway in the first few months of the occupation, some Jews in Sweden returned to their homes and businesses in Norway. They thought either that they would not be harmed in Norway or that Germany was about to invade Sweden so it would not be safe there anyway.

However, under the Nazi German dictator of Norway, Josef Terboven, the border with Sweden was subsequently closed, and the Nazis commenced a systematic effort to track down and murder the Jews. First they identified all the Jews in Norway, most of whom lived in Oslo and Trondheim. Next the Germans and their Norwegian Nazi henchmen began to harass Jews and shut down their businesses and synagogues. The final step of rounding up the Jews and sending them to the death camps in Germany and Poland was not far away.

Early in World War II, British Prime Minister Winston Churchill came up with a plan called Operation Jupiter, a proposed Allied invasion of Northern Norway. As part of the plan, in 1941 and 1942 the British secretly sent Norwegian commandos, weapons, ammunition, explosives, and other supplies by fishing boats to southern Nordland in Northern Norway. There the commandos built up a large underground organization and recruited many people to carry the supplies inland where they were stored at the Tangen farm next to a lake called Majavatn. When the planned Allied invasion of Northern Norway began, the supplies were to be used to destroy the railroad lines from Southern to Northern Norway. That would prevent the Germans from moving troops northward to attack the Allied invasion force. As it turned out, Operation Jupiter was cancelled. The Allies never invaded Norway, and instead the Americans and the British sent troops to North Africa in Operation Torch.

In the meantime, so many Norwegians in southern Nordland were recruited to haul supplies inland that pretty soon it became common knowledge among the rest of the people who lived there. Inevitably, the Germans also figured out what was going on. In September 1942 the Nazis arrested a resistance man who was a telegraph operator in Mosjøen. Under torture, he told the Germans about the weapons storage depot at the Tangen farm.

On September 6, 1942, German soldiers rowed a boat across the lake called Majavatn towards the farm, and on the way they were spotted by four Norwegian commandos. The commandos hid in the woods, and the Germans found the weapons that were stored there. When the Germans started rowing back across the lake, the Norwegian commandos opened fire, and three of the Germans were killed.

In October Terboven ordered violent reprisals in response to the killings at Majavatn and other resistance activities in Trøndelag and Nordland. Approximately 100 men from the surrounding area were arrested and sent to Falstad concentration camp north of Trondheim, where 23 of them were summarily executed. In addition, 10 prominent residents of Trondheim were pulled from their homes and shot even though they had nothing to do with the events at Majavatn. Other Norwegians were tortured and sent to concentration camps in Norway and Germany for the balance of the war. Terboven declared martial law in Trondheim, Trøndelag, and southern Nordland, and the Germans arrested all of the Jewish men they could find in Trondheim.

The arrest of the Jews in Trondheim was a clear signal to the remaining Norwegian Jews that they were no longer safe in Norway. About 150 Jews fled the country to Sweden. But for various reasons the other Jews did not go into hiding. Some were afraid of being caught trying to escape. Others were reluctant to leave their families behind and possibly subject them to arrest and reprisals. Still others felt they were too old or sick to move. Finally, there were some who did not take the threat seriously.

On October 23, 1942, the Norwegian resistance learned that the Nazis intended to arrest the remaining Jewish men on the following day. That night, resistance members alerted as many Jews as possible, and this time several hundred Jews left their homes and went into hiding. The following day the Norwegian Nazis arrested the rest of the Jewish men they could find. A month later, on November 24, they returned to arrest Jewish women and children. Later that day, at the harbor in Oslo, hundreds of Jewish men, women, and children were loaded onto a German ship called the *Donau* for a voyage to Stettin, Germany. From there they were transported to the death camps at Auschwitz and Birkenau, where almost all of them were murdered. More Norwegian Jews shared the same fate over the next several months.

During the same period of time, the Germans were escalating their efforts to pursue and arrest members of the Norwegian resistance, and hundreds of them also went into hiding in Norway. So in the last three months of 1942, there were well over 1,000 Jews and members of the underground living at secret locations in and around Oslo, and all of them were in mortal danger of being arrested and executed by the Nazis. Many stayed with friends and friends of friends, all of whom were taking a terrible risk because it was a death sentence if the Nazis found them harboring fugitives. All of the fugitives were hoping to find a way to get across the border to Sweden.

Up until that point, the various resistance organizations in Oslo, including the military resistance (*Milorg*), the civilian underground, and the Communists combined had transported as many as 50 to 60 people per week to Sweden. They were sent overland, by sea, or with false papers by rail, and many different routes were used. But the existing organizations were simply not prepared to accommodate the huge number of refugees that were now in hiding and were desperate to flee across the border. As a result, several new groups were organized to assist refugees on their way to Sweden. The newly-formed organization that assumed a major share of the responsibility for this effort was called Carl Fredriksens Transport.

At the end of October 1942, four fugitive Jewish brothers approached Rolf Syversen at his tree nursery in Oslo and asked if he could help them. Syversen hid them at the nursery and contacted a member of the resistance, who put him in touch with a man named Alf Pettersen. Pettersen was a former Norwegian policeman who had lost his job when he refused to show the necessary respect to his new Nazi superiors. Now he was working for a transport agency. He was very familiar with the border regions east of Oslo, and in fact he had already helped several fugitives to escape to Sweden. At Syversen's request, Pettersen successfully took the four Jewish brothers and later their families across the border. He was assisted by his boss at the transport agency, Reidar Larsen.

Shortly thereafter, Larsen informed Milorg leader Ole Berg what Pettersen had accomplished. On November 28 Berg sent Larsen to Pettersen to ask him to form and operate a new organization to evacuate hundreds of Jews and other Norwegians to Sweden.

Pettersen said yes, and he assembled a large team of people to assist him. They included his pregnant wife, Syversen and his pregnant wife, Larsen, a weapons expert, a student, a doctor, a dentist, a lawyer, Norwegian policemen, drivers, a group of spies who lived along the route to Sweden, lumbermen, and even some Swedish border guards. Larsen provided the trucks, and they all gathered weapons, ammunition, fuel, tarps, and other necessary supplies. Friends of Pettersen in the Norwegian passport office provided false certificates that authorized the drivers to operate in the border areas. Pettersen's wife forged fictitious transport papers for each truck, which stated that the truck was operated by a company called Carl Fredriksens Transport. It was actually a secret code name that referred to Norway's King Haakon, whose original name was Carl and whose father was King Fredrik of Denmark. All of these preparations were completed in just a matter of a few days.

Over the next six weeks until January 14, 1943, Carl Fredriksens Transport took over 1,000 refugees to Sweden by use of the following procedure. Refugees were transported from their hiding places to several safe houses in Oslo. The safe houses included a hospital, an obstetrics clinic, a dentist's office, and various residences and other buildings. Each weeknight about 40 refugees were taken by car, ambulance, or taxi to Syversen's nursery. At 8:30 p.m., two trucks arrived at the nursery. The refugees were told they could only take with them whatever each one could carry on a long walk to the border, usually just one suitcase per person. The small children were given a sleeping potion in some milk so they would sleep through the trip and not make any noise. Then the refugees and their luggage were loaded onto the back of the trucks and covered with tarps. Everyone was told to remain quiet and still.

The two trucks left the nursery at 9:00 p.m. and were driven about 60 miles in three to four hours. Pettersen's local spies along the route left inconspicuous signs on the roads to direct the drivers around Nazi roadblocks. On a few occasions, the Germans stopped the trucks, but they never looked under the tarps. Close to the border the trucks left the highway and were driven through the woods. They stopped a few hundred yards from the border. Everyone got out of the trucks, picked up their luggage, and were guided on a path through the forest to the border. Once they reached Sweden, the Swedish border guards helped the refugees to find warm shelter. Local lumbermen in Norway cut down trees and bushes to cover the truck tracks and the footprints in the snow.

The operation was financed by the Norwegian underground and by contributions from the refugees. Each refugee was asked for 150 Norwegian kroner, but those who could not afford it were actually given money to pay for food and other necessities once they got to Sweden. By December Syversen's neighbors were becoming suspicious of all the activity at the nursery, so the gathering place was moved from time to time to other locations.

After an incredibly successful six weeks, Carl Fredriksens Transport had to be shut down in mid-January because the Gestapo had gotten wind of what was going on and sent Nazi spies to infiltrate the groups of refugees. Pettersen narrowly escaped capture and fled to Sweden, as did his wife and many of his colleagues. Milorg chief Ole Berg made it to Sweden in one of the trucks. But unfortunately Syversen and others were arrested, and Syversen was executed by the Nazis in 1944. Other underground organizations continued to transport Norwegian refugees to Sweden or across the North Sea to Britain for the rest of the war.

# CHAPTER NINETEEN:
# The Missing Reindeer

*19. A Sami escapes with his reindeer in 1944.*

THE SAMI ARE THE INDIGENOUS PEOPLE of Northern Scandinavia. They speak several dialects of a Finno-Ugric language that is much different from Norwegian or any of the other Germanic languages. For many centuries, since the age of the Vikings, the Sami faced discrimination at the hands of the Norwegians. Along the coast the Sami have always been able fishermen, while the inland Sami have herded reindeer.

During the Second World War, the German occupiers of Norway considered the Sami to be a lower form of the human race. But they sometimes used the Sami as guides in the mountains of the far north, and they allowed the Sami to continue herding reindeer.

In October 1944 the Soviet Red Army crossed Norway's northern border and invaded Norway with a large force. The Germans made plans to retreat westward to the more defensible Lyngen Line near Tromsø. Under their scorched earth policy, the Germans started to burn down all buildings and destroy all other property in the areas of Norway that they abandoned. The Germans also evacuated about 50,000 Norwegians from the same areas as they retreated, and they had plans to destroy the Sami towns and villages and evacuate the Sami who lived in Finnmark.

However, the Germans knew that the Sami around the town of Kautokeino had large herds of tens of thousands of reindeer. Instead of destroying the herds, the Germans wanted the Sami to deliver the reindeer to the Lyngen Line so they could be butchered to feed the soldiers in the German army. They intended to negotiate a deal with the Sami under which the Germans would purchase the reindeer. For their part, the Sami did not want to be evacuated westward toward Lyngen, and they definitely wanted to keep their reindeer. So instead of cooperating with the Germans, the Sami came up with a secret plan to fool the Germans and escape with their reindeer.

First the Sami made excuses to delay the negotiating sessions with the Germans. Once the negotiations finally began, the Sami pretended that they could not speak Norwegian or German. The Germans had to find translators who knew both Sami and Norwegian and other translators who knew both Norwegian and German. At the negotiating table, whenever the Germans said anything, it would have to be translated into Norwegian and then into the Sami language. Whenever the Sami replied, their words were translated into Norwegian and then into German. This laborious and time-consuming procedure caused quite a delay in the entire process of working out a mutually-acceptable deal. But the

Sami were not finished with their delaying tactics. During the negotiations, they complained that they could not move the reindeer in the warm fall weather and that any attempt to move the reindeer would have to await the onset of much colder temperatures when the ground was fully frozen.

After much back and forth, the Germans and the Sami finally reached an agreement, and the Germans paid the Sami a huge sum of money to deliver the reindeer to a place called Helligskogen, which was near the Lyngen Line. As part of this arrangement, the Germans agreed to allow the Sami to evacuate their own people along with their reindeer. But before moving the reindeer, the Sami explained to the Germans that they would have to take the reindeer in separate small groups in several different directions so there would be enough grazing land to feed the reindeer on the way to Helligskogen.

At last, on November 23, 1944, after the Germans began to burn the town of Kautokeino to the ground, the Sami started to move the reindeer in many small groups. But unbeknownst to the Germans, there was another place called Helligskogen that was not west on the Lyngen Line but rather east in Finland. In the course of the next few weeks, about 1,400 Sami and all of their reindeer escaped east to Finland and Sweden, and a snowstorm covered their tracks. During the journey, if anyone asked them where they were going, the Sami said that they were on their way to Helligskogen in accordance with their agreement with the Germans.

So the Sami and all of the reindeer vanished, and the Germans did not receive any of the reindeer to feed their army. They looked for the Sami all winter, but they had no idea where they had gone. A few months later, the war ended and the Sami returned to Norway with their reindeer to rebuild their towns and villages and continue their lives.

# LIST OF ILLUSTRATIONS

Front cover: *Vår med hvit hest (The white horse in spring)* by Nikolai Astrup (1915)

1. Tune Runestone, photo by Skadinaujo (2008), Creative Commons Attribution – Share Alike 2.5 Generic license at: creativecommons.org/licenses/by-sa/2.5/legalcode

2. Viking longhouse at Avaldsnes, photo by Frank Huencke (2011), Creative Commons Attribution – Share Alike 3.0 Unported license at: creativecommons.org/licenses/by-sa/3.0/legalcode

3. Urnes stave church carving of Ragnarok, photo by Nina Aldin Thune (2012), Creative Commons Attribution – Share Alike 2.5 Generic license at: creativecommons.org/licenses/by-sa/2.5/legalcode

4. Three swords monument at Hafrsfjord, photo by Holger Uwe Schmitt (2016), Creative Commons Attribution – Share Alike 4.0 International license at: creativecommons.org/licenses/by-sa/4.0/legalcode

5. Statue of St. Sunniva, photo by Atle Råsberg (2015), Creative Commons Attribution – Share Alike 3.0 Unported license at: creativecommons.org/licenses/by-sa/3.0/legalcode

6. Nidaros Cathedral in Trondheim, photo by DXR (2015), Creative Commons Attribution – Share Alike 4.0 International license at: creativecommons.org/licenses/by-sa/4.0/legalcode

7. Ancient drawing of Bergen

8. Håkonshallen – the hall of kings in Bergen, photo by Petr Šmerkl, Wikipedia (2009), Creative Commons Attribution – Share Alike 3.0 Unported license at: creativecommons.org/licenses/by-sa/3.0/legalcode

9. Hedalen stave church in Valdres, photo by T. Bjørnstad/I, ToB (2007), Creative Commons Attribution – Share Alike 3.0 Unported license at: creativecommons.org/licenses/by-sa/3.0/legalcode

10. St. Michael's mountain on Norsjø, *St. Michaelsfjället i Telemarken* in *Nordiska taflor* (1868)

11. Steilneset Memorial in Vardø, photo by Bjarne Riesto (2011), Creative Commons Attribution 2.0 Generic license at: creativecommons.org/licenses/by/2.0/legalcode

12. Fish drying racks in Lofoten, photo by Anders Beer Wilse (1924)

13. A farm family in Gol in 1699

14. A jekt cargo ship from Nordland, photo by Frankemann (2014), Creative Commons Attribution – Share Alike 4.0 International license at: creativecommons.org/licenses/by-sa/4.0/legalcode

15. A Norwegian pioneer schoolhouse in Wisconsin, Raspberry School House, photo by Randen Pederson (2006), Creative Commons Attribution 2.0 Generic license at: creativecommons.org/licenses/by/2.0/legalcode

16. Union announcement of proposed labor agreement in 1935

17. Beautiful Ålesund, photo by Sergey Ashmarin (2014), Creative Commons Attribution – Share Alike 3.0 Unported license at: creativecommons.org/licenses/by-sa/3.0/legalcode

18 Last stretch of the road to Sweden used by Carl Fredriksens
Transport, photo by Leifern (2008), Creative Commons Attribution
– Share Alike 3.0 Unported license at:
creativecommons.org/licenses/by-sa/3.0/legalcode

19. A Sami escapes with his reindeer in 1944.

Back cover: *Gokstad* ship, Viking Ship Museum in Oslo, photo by
Karamell (2005), Creative Commons Attribution – Share Alike 2.5
Generic license at: creativecommons.org/licenses/by-sa/2.5/legalcode

# PRINCIPAL SOURCES

Allern, Tor-Helge, and Einar Niemi, eds. *Nord-Norge og 1814.* Norway: Orkana, 2015.

Alm, Ellen. *Trondheims siste heksebrenning.* Trondheim: Museumsforlaget, 2014.

Alnæs, Karsten. *Historien om Norge.* Oslo: Gyldendal, 1996-2000.

Bull, Ida, Knut Ove Eliasson, Merete Røskaft, and Steinar Supphellen, eds. *Trondheim 1814.* Norway: Fagbokforlaget, 2014.

Chartrand, R., K. Durham, M. Harrison, and I. Heath. *The Vikings: Voyagers of Discovery and Plunder.* Oxford: Osprey, 2006.

Crossley-Holland, Kevin. *The Norse Myths.* New York: Pantheon, 1980.

Dass, Petter. *Nordlands trompet.* Oslo: Gyldendal, 1996.

Grønvik, Ottar. *Runene på Tunesteinen.* Oslo: Universitetsforlaget, 1981.

Hagen, Rune Blix. *Ved porten til helvete.* Oslo: Cappelen Damm, 2015.

Hendriksen, Knut, and Mats Bäcker. *Ole Bull.* Oslo: Cappelen, 2000.

Hjardar, Kim, and Vegard Vike. *Vikinger i krig.* Oslo: Spartacus, 2012.

Hodne, Ørnulf. *Mystiske steder i Norge.* Oslo: Cappelen, 2000.

Hollander, Lee M., ed. *Old Norse poems.* New York: Columbia, 1936.

Hovdhaugen, Einar. *Husmannstida.* Oslo: Samlaget, 1975.

Hygen, Anne-Sophie, and Lasse Bengtsson. *Rock Carvings in the Borderlands.* Gothenburg: Warne, 2000.

Jaklin, Asbjørn. *Historien om Nord-Norge.* Oslo: Gyldendal, 2004.

Johansen, Elisabeth. *Brent land.* Norway: Orkana, 2013.

Jordanes. *The Origin and Deeds of the Goths.* Translated by Charles C. Mierow. Charleston, S.C.: Bibliobazaar, 2008.

Kittelsen, Th. *Svartedauen.* Kristiania: Stenersen, 1900.

Komissar, Vera. *Nådetid: Norske jøder på flukt 1942.* Oslo: Aschehoug, 1992.

Mørkhagen, Sverre. *Farvel Norge.* Oslo: Gyldendal, 2009.

Norgeshistorie.no

Næss, Hans E. *Med bål og brann.* Stavanger: Universitetsforlaget, 1984.

Roesdahl, Else. *The Vikings.* Translated by Susan M. Margeson and Kirsten Williams. London: Penguin, 1998.

Semmingsen, Ingrid. *Norway to America.* Translated by Einar Haugen. Minneapolis: University of Minnesota Press, 1978.

Skeie, Tore. *Jomfruen fra Norge.* Oslo: Spartacus, 2012.

Solberg, Bergljot. *Jernalderen i Norge.* Oslo: Cappelen, 2000.

Somerville, Angus A., and R. Andrew McDonald. *The Viking Age: A Reader.* Toronto: University of Toronto Press, 2010.

Spurkland, Terje. *I begynnelsen var futhark.* Oslo: Cappelen, 2001.

Strømsheim, Jon. *Motstandsarbeid i Ålesund, 1940-1945.* Ålesund: Aalesunds Museum, 2015.

Sturluson, Snorri. *Heimskringla.* Translated by Erling Monsen and A.H. Smith. New York: Dover, 1990.

Tacitus, Cornelius. *Germania.* Translated by Herbert W. Bernario. England: Aris & Phillips, 1999.

Tangestuen, Mats. *Carl Fredriksens Transport.* Oslo: URO/KORO, 2012.

*The King's Mirror.* Translated by Laurence Marcellus Larson. New York: The American Scandinavian Foundation, 1917.

Yilek, John A. *History of Norway.* Shelbyville, Ky.: Wasteland Press, 2015.